Amazing Phillies Feats

About the Author

Rich Westcott is the author of 26 books previous to *Amazing Phillies Feats*. A newspaper and magazine writer and editor for more than 40 years, he has written for publications throughout the country, and has appeared in 10 film documentaries about baseball, including six produced by Major League Baseball. A former player and high school coach, Rich was the founding publisher and for 14 years was editor of *Phillies Report,* a newspaper that covered the team.

The area's leading authority on Phillies history, Rich is a past president of the Philadelphia Sports Writers Association and a long-time board member. He has been inducted into four Halls of Fame. A native Philadelphian, Rich is a graduate of the William Penn Charter School, and has a bachelor's degree from Drexel University and a master's degree from Johns Hopkins University.

Amazing Phillies Feats

The Greatest Player Performances in Philadelphia Phillies History

By Rich Westcott

Foreword by Bill Giles

Copyright © 2021 by Rich Westcott

First Summer Game Books Edition 2021

All rights reserved.

No part of this publication may be reproduced, stored in a retrieval system, or transmitted in any form by any process – electronic, mechanical, photocopying, recording, or otherwise – without prior written permission from the copyright owner and the publisher. The scanning, uploading, and distribution of this book via the internet or any other means without the permission of the publisher is illegal.

Brief excerpts may be used as part of critical reviews or articles relating to the book. All inquiries should be directed to the contact information provided below.

978-1-938545-40-5 (pbk)
978-1-938545-41-2 (ebk)

For information about permissions, bulk purchases, or additional distribution, write to
Summer Game Books
P. O. Box 818
South Orange, NJ 07079

or contact the publisher at *www.summergamebooks.com*

Photos that appear in the book are property of the author, unless otherwise credited.

Dedication

To my father, W. Norris Westcott, who took me to my first Phillies game and initiated my lifelong interest in baseball. I am eternally grateful for the immense effect he had, not only on my life as a whole, but for introducing me to this very special game and ultimately a career writing about it.

And

To Dallas Green and Charlie Manuel, who performed their own brand of remarkable feats as managers of the only two Phillies teams that won a World Series. They were truly outstanding managers and the leaders of great clubs that included many of the players you're going to read about.

Acknowledgements

Write a book about a topic to which you've been connected just about all of your life, and it can be a most pleasurable experience. It certainly is for me whenever I write about baseball, especially when the subject is as extraordinary as the one on the following pages.

The subject becomes even more agreeable when you have seen all or parts of many of the events described, interviewed a number of the participants, and have a personal attachment to some of them.

Of course, *Amazing Phillies Feats* had some very helpful contributors, and I greatly appreciate what they have done to make this book a reality.

I would like to thank Bill Giles for his extremely complimentary foreword. Bill has been one of the most important people in Phillies history. Having joined the Phillies in 1969, he later served as the team's president from 1981 to 1997, has been a major stockholder, and now serves as the team's chairman emeritus. During his reign, Bill was largely responsible for turning the Phillies into one of the most successful and lucrative franchises in baseball.

A special thanks to Larry Shenk. The Phillies director of public relations for 44 years, Larry stands at the top of the list in his field. Over all the years that I've written about the Phillies, he has helped me more times than I could ever count. And his help continued when I put together this book.

I would also like to thank the players who are the subjects of chapters in this book who provided interviews, both recently and in years past. In addition, I appreciate help given to me by good friends Dan

Baker, Mark Carfagno, Dickie Noles, Bill Werndl, and the late Jack Scheuer.

Finally, I thank my lovely wife Lois for all the help she has given me, not just here, but always. As she always does, she has played a major role in the creation of this book with her encouragement, support, enthusiasm, advice, and many other kinds of help. I appreciate so very much all the things she has always done to help me, not only as a writer, but to live the wonderful life we have had together.

Other Books by Rich Westcott

- *The Phillies Encyclopedia* (with Frank Bilovsky), – three editions 1984, 1993, 2004
- *Diamond Greats – Profiles and Interviews with 65 of Baseball's History-Makers*, 1988
- *Phillies '93 – An Incredible Season*, 1994
- *Masters of the Diamond - Interviews with Players Who Began Their Careers More Than 50 Years Ago*, 1994
- *Mike Schmidt – A Baseball Legend*, 1995
- *Philadelphia's Old Ballparks*, 1996
- *No-Hitters – The 225 Games, 1893-1999* (with Allen Lewis), 2000
- *Splendor on the Diamond – Interviews with 35 Stars of Baseball's Past*, 2000
- *A Century of Philadelphia Phillies Baseball, 1900-1999*, 2000
- *Great Home Runs of the 20th Century*, 2001
- *A Century of Philadelphia Sports*, 2001
- *Winningest Pitchers – Baseball's 300-Game Winners*, 2002
- *Tales from the Phillies Dugout* (first, second, third editions), 2003, 2006, 2012
- *Native Sons – Philadelphia-Area Baseball Players Who Made the Major Leagues*, 2003
- *Mickey Vernon – The Gentleman First Baseman*, 2005
- *Veterans Stadium – Field of Memories*, 2005
- *Phillies Essential - Everything You Need to Know to be a Real Fan*, 2006

- *The Mogul – Eddie Gottlieb, A Philadelphia Sports Legend and Pro Basketball Pioneer,* **2008**
- *The Fightin' Phils – Oddities, Insights, and Untold Stories,* **2008**
- *Philadelphia Phillies – Past and Present,* **2010**
- *Back Again – The Story of the 2009 Phillies,* **2010**
- *Shibe Park/Connie Mack Stadium,* **2012**
- *Philadelphia's Top 50 Baseball Players,* **2013**
- *Great Stuff – Baseball's Most Amazing Pitching Feats,* **2014**
- *The Champions of Philadelphia – The Greatest Eagles, Phillies, Sixers, and Flyers Teams,* **2016**
- *Biz Mackey, A Giant Behind the Plate – The Story of the Negro League Star and Hall of Fame Catcher,* **2018**

Contents

Foreword by Bill Giles	xiii
Introduction	1
Billy Hamilton – The Most Runs Scored in a Season (1894)	5
Ed Delahanty – An Unmatchable Season With the Bat (1899)	11
Grover Cleveland Alexander – 16 Shutouts in One Season (1916)	17
Gavvy Cravath – Six Home Run Titles in Seven Years (1910s)	23
Cy Williams – Hit 15 Home Runs in One Month (1923)	29
Chuck Klein – Winner of the Rare Triple Crown (1933)	35
Danny Litwhiler – First Errorless Season for an Outfielder (1942)	41
Phillies Batters Slam Five Home Runs in One Inning (1949)	47
Eddie Waitkus – Came Back to Play After Getting Shot (1949-1950)	53
Richie Ashburn – The Throw That Led to a Pennant (1950)	59
Dick Sisler – 10th Inning Home Run Won a Pennant (1950)	65
Jim Konstanty – The First Reliever to Win an MVP (1950)	70
Robin Roberts – Hurled 28 Straight Complete Games (1952-1953)	76
Gene Conley – Played Two Pro Sports Simultaneously (1959-1960)	82
Art Mahaffey - Struck Out 17 Batters in One Game (1961)	89
Jim Bunning – The First Perfect Game in Team History (1963)	94

Johnny Callison – Hit All-Star Game's Greatest Home Run (1964)	100
Dick Allen – A Hitting Binge Like Few Ever Had (1966)	107
Rick Wise – A No-Hitter and Two Homers in the Same Game (1971)	112
Steve Carlton – Won 27 of the Team's 59 Victories (1972)	119
Mike Schmidt – Four Home Runs in One Amazing Game (1976)	124
Larry Bowa – A Record-Setting Year as a Shortstop (1979)	130
Tug McGraw – Strikeout Clinched First World Championship (1980)	136
Pete Rose – Set National League Record for Most Career Hits (1981)	142
Mickey Morandini – Turned Phillies' First Unassisted Triple Play (1992)	148
Mitch Williams – Drilled a Walk-off Single at 4:40 AM (1993)	154
Curt Schilling – Two Straight 300-Strikeout Seasons (1997-1998)	161
Jimmy Rollins – Hit in a Team Record 38 Straight Games (2005-2006)	166
Ryan Howard – Smashed 58 Home Runs in One Season (2006)	172
Brad Lidge – A Perfect Season as a Closer (2008)	178
Chase Utley – Blasted Five Homers in One World Series (2008)	184
Jamie Moyer – Oldest Pitcher Ever to Throw a Shutout (2010)	189
Roy Halladay – Fired Two No-Hitters in One Season (2010)	195
Sources	201

Foreword

By Bill Giles

It has been 100 years since the Giles family started their baseball careers. My father Warren Giles started in 1920 in Moline, Illinois, and I started in 1946 with the Cincinnati Reds and eventually joined the Phillies with whom I am still the chairman emeritus. Now, I am proud to have my son, Joe, working as an executive with the Phillies.

During that century, our family has been involved in virtually every aspect of the game. My father ultimately served as president of the National League and is a member of the Baseball Hall of Fame.

But if you want to ask a question about baseball, particularly Phillies baseball during those 100 years, you are probably better off asking Rich Westcott.

Westcott is a historian, a former sportswriter, editor, and publisher, and an author. You are about to read his 27th book, nine of which focus on the Phillies. His book, *The Phillies Encyclopedia*, a local bestseller, was invaluable to me during my 50 years as a Phillies executive.

Considered the leading authority on Phillies history, Rich has been involved in many writing projects with the Phillies. He was commissioned by the team to write *A Century of Phillies Baseball,* has written the chapter on the Phillies for the *Encyclopedia of Major League Baseball,* and wrote the bios for the original plaques that were hung on the Phillies Wall of Fame.

One of the things I like best about Rich is that he is truly passionate about the great game of baseball, and his writing over the years certainly reflects that description. *Amazing Phillies Feats* is a good example of that.

This is a book that covers the most remarkable individual achievements by Phillies players. There certainly have been many such feats during the team's 139-year history, but Rich has selected what he considers the most amazing ones and written a fascinating story about each of these great accomplishments.

Each one is a magnificent story, and Rich's detailed descriptions of these feats, while also profiling the players and their careers, ably demonstrate their special place in Phillies history.

Some of the stories are well known; others are not. One of the many benefits of this book is that it gives readers a first-hand look at feats performed many years ago. And the feats of Ed Delahanty and Grover Cleveland Alexander, for instance, were just as spectacular as those performed by Mike Schmidt and Ryan Howard.

All of which makes this a book that will provide fascinating reading to Phillies fans as well as to all others who have an interest in baseball's illustrious history. Truly, this is an amazing book that tells some amazing stories.

Introduction

During their 138 years, the Phillies have performed many remarkable feats. Some have been absolutely amazing. And many of them are unlike any that have ever been achieved in major league baseball.

The Phillies, of course, have had many opportunities to display greatness. After all, theirs is a franchise that began in 1883 when it joined the National League. It has played continuously in one city using one nickname longer than any other team in baseball history.

More than 2,200 players have worn the uniform of the Phillies. Some were good, some were not. Thirty-five men who played with the Phillies — either briefly or for a long time — have been inducted into the National Baseball Hall of Fame.

Phillies players have won Most Valuable Player Awards eight times. They've won seven Cy Young Awards. Ten Phils have been voted Rookie of the Year.

Nine times, Phillies hitters have won batting championships. Phillies players have also led or tied for the National League lead in home runs 26 times. Phillies pitchers have thrown 13 no-hitters. They've led or tied for the most wins in the league 17 times. And Phillies fielders have won 47 Gold Glove Awards.

Despite their lengthy existence and star players, the Phillies have won just five National League pennants and two World Series. They've been on the diamond in 13 postseasons. While that may not compare very favorably with some other big league teams, the Phillies are certainly a franchise that produced many, many memorable moments during their eventful nearly 14 decades of existence.

Over the course of the team's history, the Phillies have called five different ballparks—Recreation Park, Baker Bowl, Shibe Park/Connie Mack Stadium, Veterans Stadium, and Citizens Bank Park—their home field. They also used 25 different sites for spring training before making Clearwater their home in 1947.

Phillies players have performed numerous special feats both in their home ballparks and as visitors. Some accomplishments have been mostly forgotten and some are achievements that many Phillies followers may have never known about. Others are widely celebrated accomplishments that even today rate special attention.

Whatever they are, all are spectacular feats. And 33 of the most spectacular of these individual feats dating from the 1890s up to the 2000s are portrayed in this book.

They include Grover Cleveland Alexander firing what was even then an incredible 16 shutouts in one season. How many pitchers today even throw one shutout during a season?

Other special feats include Eddie Waitkus coming back to play after being shot by a deranged woman, Dick Sisler hitting the most famous home run in Phillies history, Gene Conley playing in MLB and the NBA at the same time, and Tug McGraw recording what was then the most famous strikeout in Phillies history.

Additional memorable feats include Robin Roberts pitching 28 straight complete games, Mike Schmidt's four home runs in a most amazing game, Mitch Williams's game-winning hit at 4:40 AM, Ryan

Howard's spectacular 58-home run season, and Roy Halladay's two no-hitters, including a perfect game, in the same season.

Among the other remarkable feats are ones achieved by Billy Hamilton, Chuck Klein, Richie Ashburn, Art Mahaffey, Johnny Callison, Dick Allen, Steve Carlton, Mickey Morandini, Jimmy Rollins, Brad Lidge, Chase Utley, and many more. All are as noteworthy as they are spectacular, and many have never been nor will they ever be duplicated.

No negative feats are included here. This is a book that focuses only on individual performances that can be celebrated, ones that put the players in a very positive light and in a very special class. Of course, there are other memorable feats that could have been included, but it is the opinion of the author that the ones written about here are the greatest in Phillies history. And by the way, this is not a book meant to include team accomplishments.

Each chapter features a brief summary of the player's background and career, in addition to a detailed account of his feat. Some of the living players were interviewed by the author, as were some who have since passed away, and other players who were teammates or opponents of the featured players were interviewed as well. Dating back to Danny Litwhiler, I have interviewed every Phillies player featured in this book.

Amazing Phillies Feats was certainly an enjoyable book to write, not only because of its focus on some of the greatest moments in Phillies history, but also because I either saw some of them in their entirety or partially, or knew the players who accomplished them.

Accordingly, this is a book that provides a close look at the greatest individual Phillies performances by some of the team's all-time greatest players. And great performances and great players they all most certainly were.

Rich Westcott, March 2021

As president of the Philadelphia Sports Writer's Association, Rich presented the 2010 National League Cy Young Award to Roy Halladay.

Billy Hamilton – The Most Runs Scored in Season (1894)

They called him "Sliding Billy." That's because he could skim into a base as well as anybody who ever appeared on a baseball field. And he did it a lot, because he was always racing from base to base.

His name was Billy Hamilton. And oh, how he could run. He could dash that stumpy 5-6, 165-pound frame around the diamond like he was chasing a bolt of lightning. It was a major part of his resume.

But he was even better with his hitting, as Hamilton was not only one of the best batters of his day, he was one of the best who ever made an appearance in the National Pastime.

Hamilton's numbers are, to put it mildly, glittering. During a 14-year career he had a batting average of .344, which ties him with Ted Williams for seventh place on the all-time list.

In 1,594 games, Hamilton scored 1,697 runs, collected 2,164 hits, stole 914 bases, and had a .455 on-base percentage. His stolen bases total ranks third on the all-time list, trailing only Rickey Henderson and Lou Brock, who played seven and five years, respectively, more than Hamilton.

He may be third now, but he was first for a long time. Once, well after his career had ended, a sports writer with *The Sporting News* referred to Hamilton as merely "one of baseball's top base-stealers." To that, Hamilton replied, "I'll have you know sir that I was and will be the greatest stealer of all time."

Also a standout bunter, Hamilton is the Phillies all-time leader in batting average (.360), on-base percentage (.468), and stolen bases (510). Hamilton spent from 1890 through 1895 with the Phillies. He broke in as a 22-year-old with the Kansas City Cowboys of the American Association in 1888, and played with the Boston Beaneaters from 1896 through 1901.

During 13 full seasons in the majors, the left-handed-hitting Hamilton hit below .300 only once, and that was in his last year when he hit .287. He hit .340 or above seven times. He stole 100 or more bases in four seasons, reaching a high of 111 two times, in 1889 and in 1891. He holds the National League record for most years (four) with 150 or more runs scored, and most combined hits and walks (349) in one season. The Newark, New Jersey native led the league in stolen bases five times, in runs four times, and in batting twice.

Along with all his superlative offensive feats, however, Hamilton did have a few flaws. He was a terrible fielder, often dropping fly balls and making poor throws. He also had a way of annoying and embarrassing his opponents with his base-running habits, including what was known as a "fadeaway slide." He also created clouds of dust as he rounded the bases, and often hurled himself into the sacks or collided with opposing infielders, sometimes knocking them over.

These practices made him a favorite of his hometown fans, but he was highly disliked by opponents' supporters. He was also extremely unpopular with opposing players. That was clearly demonstrated once when an opposing player, angry with Hamilton's antics, picked him up after he slid into third base, carried him to the stands, and threw him into the seats.

Hamilton arrived in Philadelphia in 1890, joining a team that had been badly muffled when numerous players jumped to the newly formed Players League. In his first year with the Phillies, Hamilton hit .325 and led the league with 102 stolen bases.

The following year, the Union League had folded and many of the players returned to their old teams. One was outfielder Ed Delahanty. Together, he and Hamilton, then playing left field, teamed with right fielder Sam Thompson, the National League home run leader in 1889 with a record 20 four-baggers, to give the Phillies one of the greatest outfields in big league history.

In 1891, Hamilton, often called "the human rocket," who was as fast as a deer and as slippery as an eel, won the first batting title in Phillies history with a .340 mark. He also lead the league in hits (179), runs (141), and stolen bases (111). The perfect leadoff hitter, he was on base 45 percent of his trips to the plate.

> The Phillies hit .350, by far the highest team average ever compiled. Meanwhile, Thompson hit .415 and Delahanty hit .405. Reserve outfielder Tuck Turner hit .418, playing in 80 games because of injuries to the other outfielders. And Hamilton, playing center field, hit .403.

With all three of the Phillies outfielders batting well over .300, Hamilton hit .330 in 1892, which was second in the league. Then, despite a battle with typhoid fever, he led the league with a .380 average in 1893 with Delahanty (.368) and Thompson (.370) not far behind. At one point that season, Hamilton slugged eight straight hits.

The 1894 season proved to be even better. Not only did the fabled threesome have the greatest combined performance of all time, but Hamilton put his name in the record books with a sensational season, the likes of which will never be equaled.

Billy Hamilton set a major league record when he scored 198 runs in one season.

The Phillies captured four of the top five spots in the batting race, trailing only Hugh Duffy who swatted an all-time record .440. Although they spent the early part of the season in second place, then falling in mid-season to seventh, the Phils finished in fourth with a 71-57 record, 18 games out of first. During the year, the team had to endure a fire that partially destroyed their Philadelphia Base Ball Park and forced the Phillies to play at the University of Pennsylvania's field.

In one game, the Phillies staged an unfathomable clobbering of the Louisville Colonels, 29-4. With Thompson hitting for the cycle, the Phils smashed 36 hits. Amazingly, losing pitcher Jack Wadsworth pitched the whole nine innings.

Much of the season, though, belonged to the 28-year-old Hamilton, who was playing for a salary of $1,800 for the season. He led the league in stolen bases (100), walks (128), singles (181), plate appearances (702) and on-base percentage (.521). He had 225 hits, second in the league, and career highs in runs scored (198), doubles (25) and triples (15). In one game, he stole seven bases. He also hit in 36 straight games.

The Sporting News said that "Hamilton has got base-stealing down to a science, and no player succeeds in the attempt so often in proportion to times attempted. His slide is wonderful, and often he gets away from the fielder when the latter has the ball in hand waiting to touch him."

But the biggest of all his marks was his amazing total of 198 runs scored. Not only did that rank by far at the top of the league, it stands as the most runs scored in one season in baseball history.

Hamilton, who would be inducted into the Hall of Fame in 1961, set a major league record by scoring a run in the most consecutive games (24). During that streak, he scored 35 runs. Of course, it helped that he had sluggers Thompson and Delahanty hitting behind him.

In terms of baseball records, his runs scored total is one of the most sensational marks ever recorded. And it came during a season unmatched in its entirety by any other player.

Hamilton went on to finish a standout career with the Phillies when he hit .389 while again leading the league with 166 runs scored. He also led the circuit for the fifth time in stolen bases with 97.

The 1895 season would be Hamilton's last in Philadelphia. While holding out for a modest raise salary, Phils co-owner John Rodgers showed his lack of patience when he traded Hamilton to Boston in a pathetic deal that brought them fading third baseman Billy Nash.

Hamilton went on to have six outstanding years with the Beaneaters, hitting well over .300 in all but his final season, once collecting a .369 average and in another season batting .366. One year he led the league with 152 runs scored, while crossing the plate 153 times in another season.

But it was the 1894 season that established Hamilton as baseball's greatest single-season runs scorer. It is a feat that will likely never be matched.

Ed Delahanty – An Unmatchable Season With the Bat

Anytime a batter finishes first in the leagues in a major hitting category, it is considered a special achievement. Win two or three offensive categories in a single season, and it is regarded as an even greater performance with the bat.

One of the rare batters who has done that is Ed Delahanty. The one difference between Delahanty and other hitters is that he won multiple titles during multiple seasons. But no year was more spectacular than 1899, when he hit .410 and finished first in eight offensive categories.

Delahanty carried his 40-ounce bat to the highest levels in the 1890s. Now, more than 12 decades later, his name still ranks among the greatest hitters of all time. He also stands as the greatest hitter in Phillies history.

"Big Ed," as he was called, spent 13 of his 16 big league seasons with the Phillies. Playing mostly as a left fielder, Delahanty was the biggest name on a team that for the most part was not particularly good.

Delahanty, who was inducted into the Hall of Fame in 1945, had a lifetime batting average of .346, which ranks as the fifth-highest career mark of all time. Only Ty Cobb, Rogers Hornsby, Joe Jackson, and Lefty O'Doul have higher averages.

Big Ed hit .400 or above three times, the first major leaguer ever to do that, won two batting titles and two home run crowns, led the league in RBI three times, and in slugging percentage and doubles each five times. He had 2,597 hits, and in 1,837 games scored 1,600 runs and drove in 1,466. And in the deadball era when home runs seldom made the box score, the muscular, 6-1, 170-pound right-handed slugger drilled 101 round-trippers.

One year, Ed Delahanty hit .410 and led the league in six batting categories.

With the Phillies, Delahanty hit .348 in 1,557 games. Four times he slammed at least 200 hits in a season. He drove in more than 100 runs seven times, and 10 times scored more than 100 runs, including 148 and 149 in two consecutive years. He is the Phillies' all-time career leader in triples, and ranks second in batting average, RBI, runs, and doubles, and third in total bases, stolen bases, and hit by a pitch.

A solid pull-hitter, Delahanty was the second big leaguer to hit four home runs in one game, following Bobby Lowe of the Boston Beaneaters. Once, Delahanty collected 10 straight hits. He had six hits in one game twice and eight safeties in a doubleheader. And to show he was no slowpoke, Ed reached double figures in stolen bases 15 times, including a high of 58, and hit a career total of 186 triples.

"When you pitch to Delahanty, you just want to shut your eyes, say a prayer, and chuck the ball," pitcher Freddy (Crazy) Schmit once said. "The Lord only knows what'll happen after that."

Born in 1867 in Cleveland, Ohio, Ed was the oldest of five brothers who played in the big leagues. Although brothers Frank, Jim, Tom, and Joe all played for three seasons or more—Jim played for 13 seasons and hit .283—Ed was the best of the bunch.

He once hit a ball so hard that it broke the third baseman's ankle. In addition to his brilliance with a bat, he was also an outstanding fielder, who made diving catches and possessed a rifle arm that few base runners were bold enough to test.

Originally a catcher, Delahanty began his pro career in 1887 with Mansfield of the Ohio State League. Moving up to Wheeling of the Tri State League the following year, he was hitting .412 after 21 games when the Phillies learned about his prowess as a hitter.

"You better get him quick," Phils manager Harry Wright told club president Al Reach. And so he did, buying his contract for $1,900.

Paid $300 per month, Ed was installed at second base. He hit just .228 and committed 44 errors in 67 games at 2nd. But he stole 38 bases, causing Wright to say: "He really can run. Someday, he may be a champion base-runner."

Delahanty improved to .293 in 1889, but a broken collarbone limited him to 56 games. The following year, when big league players formed their own league during a dispute with National League owners, Ed jumped to the new Brotherhood (or Players') League. He hit .296 while playing mostly shortstop with the Cleveland Infants.

The Players League folded after one season, and in 1891, Delahanty returned to the Phillies and was moved to left field. He hit only .243 but drove in 86 runs and scored 92. Unhappy with his performance, Ed decided to do something about it, and spent the winter working out every day. In 1892, he arrived at camp in the best shape of his life.

Ed's diligence paid off, and he hit .306 with 91 RBI, with a league-leading total in triples and highest slugging percentage. He followed the next year with a .368 average, and led the league in slugging and RBI (a career high 146) and 19 home runs, an extraordinary total for the era.

By then, Delahanty had become part of a history-making outfield. Consisting of Big Ed, Billy Hamilton, and Sam Thompson, the Phillies had not only three of the league's best hitters, but a threesome that would later all be inducted into the Hall of Fame. No other team has ever had three future Hall of Famers in the same outfield.

The three parlayed their greatness in 1894 into another history-making event when they all hit over .400, as did reserve outfielder Tuck Turner. Delahanty hit .405, while scoring 148 runs and collecting 131 RBI (Future Phillies manager Hugh Duffy won the batting title with an all-time record average of .440).

Delahanty hit .404 in 1895 with 106 RBI. He hit .397 in 1896, the year he became the second big leaguer to hit four home runs in one game. Two were inside-the-park blows in a 9-8 loss to the Chicago White Stockings. When Ed—who also had a single and six RBI—hit his fourth homer, Chicago pitcher Adonis Terry was among those who shook his hand when he crossed the plate. After the game, some

1,000 fans followed Delahanty to his awaiting carriage. Later, the team presented him with four cases of chewing gum—one for each home run.

The superstar continued his spectacular batting in the next two seasons, hitting .377 and .334. Then in 1899. Delahanty had not only the best year of his career, he had one of the greatest seasons any big league hitter ever had.

Delahanty led the league with a .410 batting average. His 238 hits, 55 doubles, 137 RBI, .582 slugging percentage, and total bases (338) also topped the circuit. Along with those accomplishments, he also scored 135 runs while playing in a career-high 146 games.

> During the season, he had 10 straight hits, and he hit four doubles in one game, making him the only player in baseball history to hit four home runs in one game and four doubles in another.

He also hit in 31 straight games. At the end of the season, he had led the Phillies to a third-place finish with 94 wins, the most for any Phils team until 1976.

"He created plenty of excitement for opponents and spectators when he laid his tremendous bat against a ball," wrote Robert Smith in the *New York Times.*

Despite Delahanty's and his teammates' brilliance, the Phillies never finished higher than third place, even finishing last once, in 1897. Big Ed hit .323 in 1900 and .354 the next year. In 1901, the American League was formed. After turning down an offer from Connie Mack and the Athletics, Delahanty, who had previously made a league maximum of $2,400, became one of many National Leaguers to jump to the new league when he accepted a $4,000 contract from the Washington Nationals.

Delahanty led the American League with a .376 batting average in 1902, becoming the only player in baseball history to lead both leagues in hitting, until D. J. LeMahieu accomplished the feat for the Yankees during the pandemic-shortened 2020 season, after also winning while playing for the Colorado Rockies in 2016.

Delahanty, who by then was having huge personal and financial problems, was hitting .333 in 1903 when the club suspended him, after escalating emotional and drinking problems led to his failure to show up for a game. Shortly afterward, after being put off a train for unruly behavior, his body was found at the bottom of Niagara Falls in what remains a mysterious death.

It was the end of what had been an absolutely brilliant career. Nothing contributed more to that description than his amazing season in 1899, the greatest single-season performance in the Phillies' long history.

Grover Cleveland Alexander – 16 Shutouts in One Season (1916)

There was a once a time when a shutout was an accomplishment sought after by every starting pitcher, and cherished by both the pitcher and his team.

Not anymore. Shutouts—and complete games—are as rare as twi-night doubleheaders. In the past, individual pitchers racked up more shutouts in a season than a pitching staff nowadays typically total for the entire season.

All of which makes Grover Cleveland Alexander's record of 16 shutouts in one season so phenomenal. It's a record that has never been closely approached, and the way the game is played today, it never will be.

Alexander achieved many outstanding feats during a career that was rewarded by his induction into the Hall of Fame in 1938, one of the first players to be elected. His 373 career wins are tied with Christy Mathewson as the third most wins in baseball history. He won 30 or more games three straight years. He pitched more than 300 innings in a season eight times, and he posted an earned run average lower than 2.00 six times. He also fired 90 shutouts during his career.

Grover Cleveland Alexander's single-season shutout record will never be matched.

"He had such an effortless motion and his fastball sneaked up on you," fellow Hall of Famer Frank Frisch once said. "You'd get set, but it would be by you in the catcher's mitt. He mixed his pitches like nobody before or since, and if you tried to guess with him, you were a cinch to lose."

Altogether, Alexander led the National League in both innings pitched and shutouts seven times, in strikeouts and complete games each six times, and in wins and earned run average five times apiece. He never won less than 19 games in his first seven seasons with the Phillies. And in 5,190 innings pitched during his career, he walked just 951 batters.

His superb control led distinguished sportswriter Grantland Rice to write: "Alexander could pitch into a tin can. His control is remarkable, the finest I've ever seen."

Amazingly, the Phils' home field was Baker Bowl, where it was only 272 feet down the right-field line from home to the wall, a miniscule distance that led to many high-scoring games and very few outstanding pitching feats.

> One of his many sensational single-season achievements occurred in 1915 when Alexander pitched the Phillies to their first National League pennant. While winning 31 games and posting a career low 1.22 ERA, Alexander hurled four one-hitters and three two-hitters. In one of those games, a no-hitter was erased by a two-out single in the ninth inning.

Four one-hitters in one season? Absolutely phenomenal. The only thing better during a 20-year career filled with many great accomplishments was the record compiled by Ol' Pete, as they called him, in 1916.

Born in Elba, Nebraska, one of 13 children, Alexander, who developed his ability by throwing rocks at squirrels and rabbits on his family's farm, had connections to two United States presidents. He was named after one (Grover Cleveland). The other, actor and future president Ronald Reagan, played Alexander in the movie, *The Winning Team*.

Alexander was playing minor league ball in Syracuse when the Phillies discovered him. He immediately impressed scout Patsy O'Rourke, who was in Syracuse to look at another pitcher.

When asked about Alexander, O'Rourke told Phillies owner Horace Fogel that he saw, "one of the greatest pitching prospects I've ever looked at." To that he added, "All I can say is that you better grab this Alexander before anybody else does."

After having won 29 games in 1910 at Syracuse, the Phillies bought Alex for $750, and signed him to a $1,500 contract. In his rookie season in 1911, the 24-year-old, 6-1, 185-pound righthander, posted a 28-13 record. After three more years, when Alex won 22 and 27 games in two of those seasons, the 1915 campaign arrived.

It was a glittering season for the Phillies and for Alexander. With a 31-10 record, he led the league in wins, won-lost percentage (.756) ERA (1.22), complete games (36), innings pitched (376.1), strikeouts (241), and shutouts (12), which tied Christy Mathewson's single-season record.

With his fourth one-hitter of the season—the only hit coming off the bat of Alex's former roommate Sherry Magee in the fourth inning—he beat the Boston Braves 5-0, to give the Phillies the pennant. He then downed the Boston Red Sox in the first game of the World Series, 3-1, retiring a young pinch-hitter named Babe Ruth in the ninth inning. It was the Phillies only win of the Fall Classic, and they would not win another Series game for 65 years.

Alexander's amazing exploits continued in 1916. While posting a 33-12 record, he led the league in wins, ERA (1.55), games started (45), complete games (38), innings pitched (389), hits (323), and strikeouts (167). He also pitched in relief three times. And with his league-leading number of shutouts (16), Ol' Pete set a record that has never before or since been approached.

That season, the defending National League champs were in a tight race with the Braves, Brooklyn Dodgers, and New York Giants. The Phillies had a standout team that included first baseman Fred Luderus, and outfielders Possum Whitted, Dode Paskert, and Gavvy Cravath.

Alexander beat the Giants 5-4 on opening day, then blanked the Braves on four hits in a 4-0 win before finishing the month with three wins and one loss.

He then hurled four shutouts in May while winning eight straight games. They included a three-hit, 5-0 victory over the Cincinnati Reds, a four-hit, 3-0 blanking of the Pittsburgh Pirates, and an eight-hit, 1-0 victory over Brooklyn. He followed in June with a single whitewash, a nine-hit, 2-0 win over the St. Louis Cardinals. In a 2-1 win against the Pirates, he lost a shutout in the ninth inning when a line drive by Honus Wagner bounced off Alexander's leg and scored a run.

Taking a 13-3 record into July, Alexander hurled three more shutouts, including a two-hit, 6-0 win over Cincinnati. In another game that took just one hour and 18 minutes to play, he shut out the Pirates on four hits in a 4-0 triumph.

By the start of August, Alexander had won 19 games. And in another fabled month, he tossed four shutouts. In one, he went the distance in a 12-inning, 1-0 victory over the Chicago Cubs. He also downed the Reds 1-0 on a three-hitter.

Alexander began September with a 3-0 win over Brooklyn. Then late in the season, he pitched both games of a doubleheader, beating the Braves 7-3, in the opener and 4-0 in the nightcap.

Ol' Pete's last start was three days before the season ended, a three-hit, 2-0 win over Boston in a game that took one hour and 20 minutes that gave him his 33d win. His only other trip to the mound that year was his third relief appearance of the season, a 7-5 win over the Braves.

Thus, Alexander had completed a legendary season. Of course, it was not his last one. He had his third straight 30-win season in 1917, recording a 30-13 record and tossing eight shutouts.

Following that season, the Phillies traded Alex to the Cubs in a highly questionable swap. The explanation given by Phils owner Horace Baker was that he feared that the ace pitcher would be drafted into World War 1, and accordingly, he wanted to get something for him before that happened.

By then, Alexander was having some problems of his own. He had developed epilepsy, which caused seizures. He was also a heavy drinker, a condition that began when he was a young pitcher.

Drafted into the Army, Alexander spent most of the 1918 season serving as an infantryman in France. He returned in 1919 and pitched a little more than seven years with the Cubs, posting 27-14 and 22-12 records along the way.

The Cubs sent Alexander to St. Louis in 1926, where he recorded a famous strikeout of the New York Yankees Tony Lazzeri with the bases loaded in the ninth inning of the seventh game to give the Cardinals their first World Championship. Alex had a 21-10 season the following year, then in 1930 returned briefly to the Phillies, appearing in nine games with no wins and three losses.

That was Alex's last season. He had spent 20 superb seasons in the majors. None, however, equaled his feat in 1916 when he threw 16 shutouts, a record that is unimaginable to fans of the contemporary game.

Gavvy Cravath – Six Home Run Titles in Seven Years (1910s)

Back before the home run was considered baseball's chief offensive weapon, before Babe Ruth became a long-distance clouter, even before there was a lively ball, there was Gavvy Cravath.

Cravath opened a whole new way the game was played. He popularized the home run, made it an everyday part of the game, and when he did, baseball was never again the same.

Ruth, with his prodigious smashes, brought the game out of the deadball era. But it was Cravath who got the ball rolling. Given his record, he can be considered the father of the modern home run.

Cravath was the last and most prolific long-ball hitter of the deadball era. While playing with the Phillies, he won six National League home run championships in seven years, the most in the game's history to that point.

Cravath hit 24 home runs in 1915, to that point, the most ever by a player in the 20th century.

Cravath twice led the league in RBI, slugging average and total bases, and once in hits, runs, and walks. He homered in double figures six times and hit .280 or above in all but one year with the Phillies, from 1912-1920. He finished his 11-year big league career with a .287 batting average, 119 home runs, and 719 RBI. All but two of his four-baggers were stroked while with the Phillies.

Quite obviously, it was as a home run hitter that Cravath was mostly known, as evidenced by Robert (Tiny) Maxwell, at the time a prominent sportswriter and editor of the *Philadelphia Public Ledger*. "Gavvy is the greatest home run clouter in the history of baseball," Maxwell wrote. "He has piled up a record that might never be equaled."

Gavvy Cravath was the first prolific home run hitter in the 20th century.

The record, of course, was soon equaled. Cravath's 24 home run season was eclipsed in 1919 by Ruth, who hit 29 homers and also erased Cravath's record of six home run titles with his seventh crown in 1926. In the National League, it took until 1952 for the record to be surpassed, by Ralph Kiner of the Pittsburgh Pirates, who led the senior circuit in long balls the first seven years of his career.

Cy Williams set a new club record for the Phillies in 1922 with 26, and two years later set a new career team record, passing Cravath's 117. Cravath was born in Escondido, California, and while playing semipro baseball in Mexico, picked up the nickname of Gavvy. According to various reports, Cravath hit a ball that struck and killed a seagull. The fans in attendance yelled "gaviota," the Spanish word for seagull. From that word, sports writers came up with Gavvy.

Cravath joined the pro ranks in 1903, playing for the Los Angeles Angels in the Pacific Coast League. He was originally a catcher, but soon switched to playing right field and first base.

"Catchers were a drag on the market," he said. "They needed outfielders really bad. They told me that any catcher could play the outfield. So I did."

Cravath broke into the majors in 1908, and after transferring to right field, played briefly with the Boston Red Sox, where he picked up his second nickname "Cactus" because of his prickly personality. He also spent time with the Chicago White Sox and played three games for the Washington Senators in 1909 before getting sent down to the minor league's Minneapolis Millers.

After leading the American Association in home runs twice (once with 29, up to that point, the most ever hit in professional baseball) and in batting average (.363), Cravath, now 31 years old, was sold for $4,000 to the Phillies.

Becoming the team's starting right fielder in 1912, Cravath, who had been in an out of the minor leagues for nearly one decade, hit .284 with 11 homers and 70 RBI. The following year, he hit .341 and won his first home run title with 19 while also leading the National

League with a then-NL record 128 RBI, hits (179), and slugging percentage (.568), and hit a career-high 34 doubles.

That year, Cravath finished second in the voting for the Chalmers Award, the era's equivalent of today's Most Valuable Award, although many thought that he should have won the honor instead of batting champion Jake Daubert of Brooklyn.

Over the next two years, Cravath continued his sparkling pace, leading the league each season in home runs. In 1914, he hit .299 with 100 RBI, and 19 homers—all coming at Baker Bowl. He also led NL outfielders with 34 assists.

In contrast to his hitting, Cravath was considered extremely slow afoot.

> "They call me wooden shoes, piano legs, and a few other names," he said. "I do not claim to be the fastest man in the world, but I can get around the bases with a fair wind and all sails set. So long as I am busting the old apple on the seam, I am not worrying a great deal about my legs."

Although he batted right-handed, the 5'-10½", 186-pound Cravath sometimes utilized Baker Bowl's short right-field wall, which then stood just 272 feet down the first base line. The left field wall was a normal 340 feet from home plate.

Cravath would always think of himself as a power hitter. When asked about that lofty position and his distaste for singles hitters, he said: "Short singles are like left-hand jabs in the boxing ring, but a home run is a knockout punch. It is the clean-up man of the club that does the heavy scoring work, even if he is wide in the shoulders and slow on his feet.

"There is no advice I can give in batting except to hammer the ball," he added. "Some players steal bases with hook slides and speed. I steal bases with my bat."

And he did. In 1915, Cravath, drove the club to its first pennant, hitting .285 while leading the league in home runs (24), RBI (115), runs (89), and slugging average (.510). It was a season in which Cravath was by far the only power hitter on the team, with only one other player swatting homers in double figures (Beals Becker with 11).

During the season, he tied a club record with eight RBI in one game on four doubles in a 14-7 decision over the Cincinnati Reds. Then on September 29, he hit a three-run homer in the first inning, and in the seventh, doubled and scored. Combined with a one-hitter hurled by Grover Cleveland Alexander, the two stars led the Phillies to their first National League pennant with a 5-0 win over the Boston Braves.

But the Phillies, who drew a dazzling crowd of 449,898 during the regular season, which was more than triple that of the previous campaign, won only one game against the Red Sox in the World Series. Cravath drove in the winning run in the Phillies' 3-1 victory in Game One with a bases-loaded ground out, but he got only two hits in the entire Series.

Cravath continued to pound the ball in the next two seasons, hitting .283 and .280 and tying for the home run crown in 1917 with 12. He won home run titles in 1918 and 1919 with eight and 12, respectively, but his playing time was being increasingly reduced. At 38 years old, he wound up with just 214 at-bats in 1919, but hit .341.

By then, though, Gavvy's baseball career had taken a major detour. When Jack Coombs was fired in mid-season as the Phillies' manager after winning just 18 of 63 games, Cravath was given the job. Cravath's 1919 Phillies posted a 29-46 record, and the team finished last. The following year, with Cravath replacing himself in right with a youngster named Casey Stengel, the Phils were last again with a 62-91 mark. Cravath, who led the league with 12 pinch-hits, was dismissed at the end of the season.

In the end, though, that hardly mattered. Cravath had etched his name in Phillies history with the club's greatest home run championship streak of all-time. No one before or since won that many home run titles in such a short time.

Cy Williams – Hit 15 Home Runs in One Month (1923)

Even after the lively ball came along in the early days of the 1920s, home run hitters were still relatively uncommon. The home run hadn't quite found its place as a major factor in baseball games.

Of course, there was Babe Ruth. When it came to hitting home runs, he was the one four-bag clouter who dominated the headlines.

There was another batter, however, who earned a place among the leading homer hitters of the era. His name was Cy Williams, and some of his long-distance feats with the bat proved to be in a class by themselves.

Williams won or shared three home run crowns with the Phillies and four altogether. One of those seasons was absolutely remarkable. With it, Williams earned a special place in not only Phillies but also major league baseball's home run history.

In 1923, Williams became only the second batter in National League history to hit more than 40 home runs in a season when he smacked 41 round-trippers. Only Rogers Hornsby with 42 homers in 1922 – a year in which he batted .401 – had hit more than 40 home runs before Williams. (Ruth had done it in the American League with 54 homers in 1920 and 59 in 1921). Moreover, no one on the Phillies hit as many homers in one season as Williams did in 1923 until Mike Schmidt banged 45 into the seats in 1979.

The left-handed Williams not only had a memorable season, he also had a remarkable feat in May. In that month, he slammed 15 home runs, then a National League record for most homers hit in one month. From the start of the season until June 1, Williams belted 18 homers, which in the National League has only been matched by Willie Mays and Tony Perez. In May, Williams also collected 44 RBI, still a Phillies record for one month.

Few hitters in his era hit home runs as often as Cy Williams did.

Williams, who also became the first National Leaguer to hit 200 homers in his career, spent 19 seasons in the big leagues, including a little more than five years with the Chicago Cubs starting in 1912. (He never played in the minor leagues.) With the Cubs, he hit 13 homers in 1915, six of which were inside-the-park, and in 1916, he tied with Dave Robertson of the New York Giants for the NL lead in homers with 12.

The native of Wadena, Indiana and a graduate of Notre Dame University where he majored in architecture and played football for the legendary coach, Knute Rockne, came to the Phillies in 1918 via one of the greatest trades in team history. The Phils swapped aging outfielder Dode Paskert for Williams.

Williams went on to spend 13 seasons with the Phillies, during which time he was unquestionably the best player for a club that languished in the doldrums of the National League. Playing at Baker Bowl with a right-field wall that by then stood just 280 feet from home plate, the 6-2, 180-pounder was a dead pull-hitter who took advantage of the short distance with great frequency.

With the Philllies, Williams hit 217 home runs while batting .306 with 1,553 hits and 795 RBI in 1,463 games. He hit over .300 six times. Currently, he ranks in the top 10 of Phillies career batting records in home runs, batting average, hits, total bases (2,539), and slugging percentage (.500).

He also smacked nine grand-slam homers and hit for the cycle twice (1922 and 1927). He still holds a club record nine pinch-hit home runs during his career in Philadelphia.

Along the way he hit .328 in 1924, .331 in 1925, and .345 in 1926 when he finished fourth in the batting race. That year, he led the league with a .568 slugging percentage.

When he retired after the 1930 season at the age of 42, Williams compiled a career .292 batting average with 251 home runs, 1,981 hits, 1,005 RBI, 1,024 runs scored, and a .470 slugging percentage.

Williams was not only a masterful home run hitter, he was also a brilliant fielder. One of the premier center fielders in the game, *The Sporting News* once called him "the best fly catcher in the league." He was also noted by the *South Bend Tribune* as "the fastest runner in the national game."

The term "Williams Shift" was said to have first been applied to Ted Williams. Not so. Cy was such a strong pull hitter that teams often moved all three outfielders to the right side of the field, and three of the four infielders between second and first base.

"I couldn't hit a ball to left if my life depended on it," Williams once said. Nevertheless, the shift never bothered him. Williams was regarded as the National League's home run king of the 1920s.

Starting with the Phillies in 1920, Williams led the league in home runs with 15 while setting a career-high with 192 hits. He hit 18 and 26 homers over the next two seasons, which placed him third and second in the league.

Then, in 1923, he had a season that was considered one of the most remarkable in Phillies history. From May 1 through May 31, Williams had a month that was simply magnificent.

On the first day of the month, he bashed two home runs, plus a double, a single, and collected four RBI in a 12-10 win over the Brooklyn Robins. Then from May 3 through May 9, he homered in each of the four games. In one game, he smashed four hits, including a home run and two doubles while driving in four runs, but the Phillies lost to the Giants, 11-9.

On May 11, the Phillies won one of their most memorable games, beating the St. Louis Cardinals, 20-14. In a game in which there were 10 home runs hit, the Phils collected 18 hits, including three four-baggers by Williams, who drove in seven runs. One of Williams's blasts was a grand slam. It was only the third time since 1900 that a major leaguer hit three home runs in one game.

Afterward, Williams hit seven home runs in games between May 12 and May 24. One of the round-trippers came against Grover Cleveland Alexander, then pitching for the Cubs, in a 7-4 Phillies loss.

On May 27, Williams homered, hit two singles, and drove in three runs in a 12-4 loss to the Giants. That would be Williams's 15th home run of the month, setting a Phillies record that many years later was matched in 2004 by Jim Thome.

Williams went on to finish May with 38 hits and 44 RBI, the most RBI in one month in Phillies history. Only four times during the month did he go hitless in a game. Unfortunately, the Phillies lost 10 of the 12 games in which Williams homered.

Despite Williams's heroics, the Phillies posted a 50-104-1 record that season, finishing in last place for the fourth time in five years. It would have been a lot worse, though, if Williams hadn't been there.

> Loyal and dedicated, Williams never complained about his team's ineptitude. "I couldn't do that," he once said. "I've always received a square deal in Philadelphia. I couldn't do less than give the club a square deal in return, could I?"

Along with his home run crown, he finished the 1923 season batting .293, with 157 hits in 535 at-bats. Williams collected a career-high 114 RBI playing in 136 games. His RBI and total bases (308) total placed second in the league and his .576 slugging percentage ranked third. He was also the first Phillies batter to swat 40 or more homers and drive in at least 100 runs in one season.

Williams won one more home run crown in 1927 when he tied the Cubs' Hack Wilson with 30 dingers. That year, he became the first Phils hitter to homer in four straight games.

At age 39, Williams was the oldest player ever to lead the league in home runs. The stalwart slugger spent his last three years with the Phillies, primarily as a pinch-hitter. During that time, he hit nine home runs and collected 24 hits in 74 at-bats as a pinch-hitter, good for a .324 average.

Williams retired after the 1930 season at the age of 42. He posted some super numbers. None was better, though, than the ones he recorded in 1923, especially during the month of May.

Chuck Klein – Winner of the Rare Triple Crown (1933)

In the annals of baseball, winning a Triple Crown is a super-extraordinary accomplishment. It almost never happens, but when it does, it puts the batter into a highly celebrated class of hitters.

Going back to major league baseball's beginnings, there been only 17 Triple Crown winners. Most of the game's greatest sluggers are absent from the list. One who isn't is Chuck Klein. One of the Phillies greatest batsmen, Klein led the National League in hits, home runs, and RBI in 1933, a year that was the greatest of five straight glittering ones for the smooth-swinging slugger, who was inducted into the Hall of Fame in 1980.

Ironically, in an era when five cities had teams in both the National and American Leagues, not only did the 6-0, 190-pound Klein win the Triple Crown in 1933, so did Jimmie Foxx of the Philadelphia Athletics. It was the only time batters from the same city won Triple Crowns in each league in the same year.

Klein's Triple Crown, the only one by a Phillies hitter, stands as one of the greatest single seasons in club history. Appropriately, Klein was one of the greatest hitters in club history.

Chuck Klein holds his MVP trophy earned in 1932.

During a 17-year career, Klein had a batting average of .320, with 2,076 hits, 300 home runs, 1,168 runs scored, 1,201 RBI, and a slugging percentage of .543. Klein led the league in home runs four times; in runs scored three times; in games played, hits, doubles, and RBI twice; and in batting average and stolen bases once. All came during his first six years in baseball when he played with the Phillies.

While playing 15 years with the Phillies, Klein hit .326 with 243 home runs, 1,705 hits and 983 RBI. He ranks fourth in club history in batting average and RBI, and fifth in home runs.

Along with these hitting accomplishments, Klein was in the starting lineup in the first two All-Star games. Twice during his career, he hit for the cycle. He was also the first National League player in the 20th century to slam four home runs in one game.

> Even to this day, Klein holds a collection of National League records. He holds the mark for most total bases by a left-handed batter in one season (445), most RBI by a lefty in one season (170), most consecutive years of 400 or more total bases (three), and most games with one or more hit in a season (135). There was not much Klein couldn't do with his bat.

He is also tied for National League records for most consecutive years leading the league in total bases (four), most runs scored in two straight games (eight), most extra-base hits by a left-handed batter in one season (107), and most consecutive years leading the league in runs (three).

A native of Indianapolis, Indiana, Klein was playing in 1928 with the Ft. Wayne Chiefs in the Class B Central League when the Phillies bought his contract in mid-season for $5,000. Klein joined the Phils during what would be three straight last-place finishes.

When Klein arrived at the Phillies clubhouse, he introduced himself to manager Burt Shotten. Looking at the big, gawky kid, Shotten said: "They tell me you can hit. Goodness knows we need hitters."

And that's exactly what the Phillies got. In 64 games and playing right field, Klein hit .360 with 11 homers and 34 RBI. In 1929, he hit .356 with 145 RBI and a league-leading and career-high 43 home runs, at the time the highest in National League history. Then the following year he hit a walloping .386 with 40 homers and 170 RBI.

The Phillies home field in those days was Baker Bowl, where it was only 280 feet down the right field line from home plate to a 40-foot high wall. Throughout his career, Klein would be belittled by critics who would claim that his home runs were too easy and were not really legitimate four-baggers. That was a phony claim, however, because many of Klein's home runs flew high over the wall and out into Broad Street where the windshields of cars driving by were often smashed.

Nevertheless, claiming that "home runs have become too cheap" at the ballpark, owner William Baker had a 20-foot screen placed atop the wall. It was often said by Baker's detractors, however, that the reason he heightened the wall to 60 feet was so Klein wouldn't hit as many home runs and therefore not demand a bigger salary.

This controversy not withstanding, Klein continued his magnificent spree in 1931, hitting .337 while leading the league with 31 home runs and 121 RBI. In 1932, he had another smashing season, going .348-38-137, again leading the NL hits (223) and in four-baggers, becoming the first player in the modern era to lead the league in home runs and stolen bases (20). He was named the year's Most Valuable Player. With his red-hot bat, Klein led the Phillies to a fourth-place finish. It would be the team's only first division finish during a 31-year period from 1918 to 1949.

Then came 1933, when he had another absolutely amazing season. It would turn out to be the fifth of five straight spectacular seasons for Klein as his 42-ounce bat exploded with astonishing regularity.

In May, he hit for the cycle for the second time in a 14-inning game with the St. Louis Cardinals. By the end of June, he had hit 24 home runs, more than any National League had ever hit up to that date. He became the starting right fielder in the first All-Star Game, and the first Phillies player ever to bat in one. During the season, he smacked three grand-slam home runs, hit for the cycle for the second time in his career, and led NL outfielders with 21 assists.

Klein finished the season leading the league in batting average (.368), home runs (28), RBI (120), hits (223), doubles (44), slugging average (.602), on-base percentage (.422), and total bases (365). His batting excellence was joined by his superb ability as a baserunner and fielder.

In winning the Triple Crown, Klein joined a distinguished group that included Nap Lajoie, Ty Cobb, and Rogers Hornsby, who did it twice. Since Klein's and Foxx's entry into that group, a Triple Crown has been won only eight more times, the last by Miguel Cabrera in 2012.

Unbelievably, Klein finished second in the MVP voting to New York Giants pitcher Carl Hubbell, who had posted a 23-12 record and hurled his team to a World Series victory.

Meanwhile, Foxx had won the Triple Crown with a .356 batting average, 48 home runs, and 163 RBI. For Foxx, it was one of many brilliant seasons that would lead to his induction into the Hall of Fame.

On November 21, 1933, the Phillies made one of the most unfathomable moves in team history. They traded Klein to the Chicago Cubs for three aging and low-level players and $65,000. After five and one-half brilliant years in Philadelphia, Klein was gone. Phillies followers were outraged.

Klein had some decent seasons with the Cubs, but not even close to what he did as a Phillie. Then in 1936, in another strange move, Klein was traded back to the Phillies. He hit .309 for the season, and hit four home runs in a 10-inning game in which the Phils beat the Pittsburgh Pirates, 9-6.

Klein played parts of four seasons with the Phillies, hitting as high as .325 in 1937, but he was released during the 1939 season and picked up by the Pirates. Pittsburgh released him at the end of that season, and Klein returned to the Phillies for his third stint with the team.

With World War ll calling numerous big league players to military service, Klein stayed with the Phillies for the next five years, playing sparingly in his last three seasons. Along the way, the Phillies made him a coach. Klein retired after the 1944 season. It had been a sparkling career for the esteemed slugger, certainly one of the greatest in Phillies history. Especially the great 1933 season, when Klein had one of the greatest seasons in Phillies history.

Danny Litwhiler – First Errorless Season for an Outfielder (1942)

Nobody ever said that playing the outfield was easy. Balls come out at all different speeds, distances, levels, and angels. And throws must be made accurately.

Danny Litwhiler is one who could attest to all of that. He was a major league baseball player for 11 years, performing with the Phillies, St. Louis Cardinals, Boston Braves, and Cincinnati Reds, compiling a lifetime batting average of .281 with 982 hits, and playing in 1,057 games, from 1940 to 1951. With the Phillies, he posted a .291 batting average with 425 hits and 156 RBI in 374 games.

It was on defense, though, that Litwhiler performed one of the most noteworthy fielding achievements, not only in Phillies history, but at the time, in the entire history of big league baseball.

In 1942, his third season with the Phillies, Litwhiler, 25 years old at the start of the season, became the first outfielder in major league history to play a full season of 150 or more games without making an error.

With rickety future Hall of Famer Lloyd Waner playing much of the season in center field, left fielder Litwhiler was forced to cover a large territory in the outfield, and he performed perfectly: in 151 games (three others were rained out) he fielded 317 chances, making 308 putouts and adding nine assists without a single bobble.

And to add to this amazing feat, Litwhiler extended his streak the following season to 187 straight games without an error, playing every inning of every game. He made just one error during the season. Today, his glove is on display at the Baseball Hall of Fame in Cooperstown, New York.

"You have to be very lucky to do what I did," Litwhiler said many years later. "You can make a perfect throw, but it could hit something and take off or it could hit the guy sliding in and you would get an error.

While playing in 151 games one season, Danny Litwhiler committed zero errors.

"You have to have good hands, too. And you have to learn to block the ball. I could have been given some errors, but by moving in close and blocking the ball, I didn't get charged with errors because I was able to prevent the runner from moving up a base.

"The irony of my fielding record," the 5-10, 198-pound Litwhiler recalled "is that I went from worst to first. The previous year, I led National League outfielders with 15 errors."

Litwhiler, however, had hit .305 that year with a career-high 18 home runs, including at least one homer in every National League ballpark. Then in 1942, he batted just .271, but led the Phillies in batting average, runs (59), hits (160), at-bats (591), games played (151), doubles (25), triples (9), home runs (9), and RBI (56). He was also named to the National League's All-Star team.

No player has either before or since led the Philllies in that many categories in the same season. Of course, factoring into that may be the Phillies' last place finish that year with a 42-109 record, the fifth straight year the team had lost more than 100 games. The Phils had a team batting average of .232 and finished 62 ½ games out of first place.

Litwhiler's fielding record was by far the only noteworthy achievement on the team that quite obviously was downright awful. It was hailed throughout baseball as a sensational piece of work that ranked far above the usual fielding record of previous big league outfielders. Ironically, there were a couple plays that almost prevented it from happening.

In one, Stan Hack of the Chicago Cubs hit a ball down the left field line. "I went over to block the ball," Litwhiler remembered, "but it hit something and started to get by me. I stuck my foot out and blocked it, then picked up the ball and threw Hack out at second. I almost had an error that time."

Late in the season, Litwhiler was actually charged with an error in a game against the New York Giants at the Polo Grounds. It had been raining and there was a big puddle in left field. Johnny Mize hit a line drive to left and Litwhiler made a shoestring catch. Meanwhile, Willard Marshall was running from second base, and Litwhiler figured that since Marshall had left the base early, he could throw him out at second.

"Just as I went to plant my feet to throw," Litwhiler said, "I hit the water. My feet went out from under me, and I slid about 20 feet. Water was flying everywhere, and I dropped the ball. I looked up and saw a big E on the scoreboard."

The next day Litwhiler looked at game stories in several newspapers, and there was no error in the box score. His errorless season was therefore still intact and would stay that way for the rest of the campaign. But Litwhiler had no clue as to why there had been a change in the call.

"About 10 years later, I'm at a banquet in New York and Mel Allen says to me, 'Remember the season you fielded 1.000? Do you know how you did it?' I told him I had a lot of luck."

According to Allen, after the game Mize had rushed in his uniform up to the press box to see the official scorekeeper. "How can you give that kid an error on a play like that," he roared.

"Here I am trying to hit .300. Hitting is my bread and butter, and I'm hitting .299, and you take a hit away from me."

The scorekeeper told Mize that he thought it was a legitimate error. "What do you think?" the scorer asked Allen, who was standing nearby. Allen said he thought it was a hit, and the scorekeeper changed his call from an error to a hit. "All those years, and I never knew what had happened," Litwhiler said.

Litwhiler's streak finally ended at Shibe Park in 1943 near midseason when a ball hit a divot on the ground and he tried to stop it with his bare hand, but it bounced past him. He was given an error, the only one charged to him all season.

In one of their many bad trades of that era, Litwhiler was shipped to the Cardinals during the 1943 season. He helped the Cards win World Series in that year and the next. He continued to play until he retired after 1951 when he was both a player and a coach with the Reds.

During a career spent entirely in baseball, Danny Litwhiler, who made just 39 errors during his entire career, had numerous accomplishments, many of which have had a lasting effect on the game.

Along with being a standout player, Litwhiler was an author, inventor, college professor, coach, manager, and he played a vital role in turning baseball into an international game.

> Among his numerous baseball- and coaching-related inventions, Litwhiler produced the Jugs Speed Gun, a widely used device that times the speed of a thrown or hit baseball, and he developed a special kind of water-resistant dirt still used on baseball diamonds. He wrote six books, including four on baseball fundamentals and one on a glossary of baseball terms translated from English into seven different languages. He was the driving force behind getting baseball included in the Olympics, a member of the U.S. Olympic Baseball Committee for 14 years, and a president of the U.S. Baseball Federation.

Litwhiler was also a professor of physical education and the head baseball coach at both Michigan State and Florida State Universities, where over a 28-year period he sent more than 100 players into professional baseball. That group included Steve Garvey, Kirk Gibson, Mike Marshall, and Dick Howser. A native of Ringtown, Pa., and a graduate of Bloomsburg University of Pennsylvania, where the baseball field is named after him, Litwhiler was also a coach with the Cincinnati Reds and a minor league manager.

Litwhiler's remarkable 1942 season has been matched eight times by Phillies outfielders, including Don Demeter, Johnny Callison, and Tony Gonzalez in the 1960s; Milt Thompson and Jim Eisenreich in the 1990s; Doug Glanville in 2002; and Shane Victorino in both 2006 and 2011. But it was Litwhiler who was the first one to set that record, and when he did, it was regarded as one of the greatest defensive feats of all time.

Phillies Batters Slam Five Home Runs in One Inning (1949)

In all of the years that the Phillies have been playing, there has never been a season quite like the one in 1949. It ranks among the most unusual in the club's 139-year history.

The 1949 season, when the Phillies finished in third place, was the first time since 1932 that they wound up in the first division in the National League. It was also only the second time since 1917 that the Phillies posted a winning record and their highest finish since that same year. During those 31 years between 1917 and 1949, the Phillies finished in last place 16 times and lost 100 or more games in 12 seasons.

On the plus side, the 1949 campaign was the first full season for Eddie Sawyer as the Phillies manager. It was also the first full season for Robin Roberts, the season when Jim Konstanty was converted into a full-time relief pitcher, and the year when Richie Ashburn and Granny Hamner tied for the league lead with a total of 662 at-bats. On the down side, it was also the year during which Eddie Waitkus was shot by a deranged woman in a hotel room in Chicago.

Joining these unusual events was the game on June 2 at Shibe Park against the Cincinnati Reds. In that game, Phillies players made history when they hit five home runs in one inning.

To add to that unusual feat, the Reds team was managed by a Philadelphia native and former Phillies player Bucky Walters. Four of the starters on that team were former Phillie Danny Litwhiler, former and future Phillie Johnny Wyrostek, and future Phillies Jimmy Bloodworth and Frankie Baumholtz. In addition, the Reds starting pitcher was Ken Raffensberger, another former Phillie who with that team had been the winning pitcher in the 1944 All-Star Game.

Only once before in National League history had a team hit five home runs in one inning. That was done in 1939 by the New York Giants in beating Cincinnati, 17-3.

The five home run barrage has since been accomplished in the National League by the San Francisco Giants in 1961 and the Milwaukee Brewers in 2006. In a great piece of irony, the opponent in all the games was the unfortunate Reds.

When the Phillies waged their slugfest, they had a 19-20 record. They were in the midst of a three-week batting slump when the Reds came to town. Nevertheless, the Phillies jumped out to a 1-0 lead in the second inning when catcher Andy Seminick slammed a solo home run.

With Curt Simmons on the mound and a crowd of just 13,777 in attendance, the lead held up until the fifth inning. Prior to that, the 20-year-old left-hander, who had been signed and given a $65,000 bonus two years earlier, had allowed only one hit, a double by Bloodworth.

In the fifth, though, the Reds took a 2-1 lead. Litwhiler laced a single and eventually came around to score on Wyrostek's single. Then Wyrostek scored on a single by Baumholtz.

The Phillies tied the score in the sixth inning when Hamner reached first on a bunt single, went to second on a walk to Seminick, and scored on Stan Hollmig's single. But Cincinnati went back ahead, 3-2, in the seventh with Ray Mueller smacking a double and scoring on Raffensberger's double. It would be the final inning for Simmons.

The Reds' lead didn't stay for long, however. In the bottom of the eighth inning, the Phillies cut loose like no Phillies team had ever done before.

At the time, the left-handed Raffensberger, who would post an 18-17 record that season for the seventh-place Reds, had a 6-3 record (which included one win over the Phillies), was firing a four-hitter. He had struck out four and walked four.

Leading off the inning was Del Ennis. A Philadelphia native, Ennis had joined the Phillies as a 20-year-old in 1946, and with a .313 batting average and 17 home runs, had been named the National League's Rookie of the Year. During an 11-year stint with the Phillies, Ennis would become one of the area's most celebrated native sons.

> On Raffensberger's first pitch, Ennis, who would bat .302 that season with 25 homers and 110 RBI, crushed it into the upper deck in left field for his seventh home run of the season. Then, on the very next pitch, Seminick drilled his second home run of the game over the roof in left field.

That was it for Raffensberger. He was replaced by Jess Dobernic, a seldom used right-hander who in 18 games that year would end up with an 11.57 ERA.

Dobernic got Hollmig to line out to Virgil Stallcup at shortstop, but Willie Jones, owner of a .244 batting average that season with 19 four-baggers and 77 RBI, followed with his third home run of the year into the lower deck in left field. Eddie Miller than popped out to Bloodworth at second.

Next up was pitcher Schoolboy Rowe, normally a starter, but who had replaced Simmons in the top of the eighth. Rowe, an outstanding hitter who was in his 15th and final season in the majors, slammed a home run into the upper deck in left field for his 18th career four-bagger.

Schoolboy Rowe, Del Ennis, Andy Seminick, and Willie Jones (l-r) hit a combined five home runs in one inning.

That gave the Phillies a 6-3 lead, but the inning was far from over. Kent Peterson, brought in to replace Dobernic, walked Ashburn, then gave up a double to Hamner that missed by about one foot going over the left field wall. Waitkus then reached base when first baseman Ted Kluszewski dropped a throw from third baseman Bobby Adams with Ashburn scoring on the error.

Batting for the second time in the inning, Ennis followed with a single to center with Hamner scoring on the hit. Then up to the plate came Seminick.

The Phillies' number 1 catcher since 1946, the rugged backstop was not a particularly feared hitter, although he did have some notable moments at the plate. In 1949 and 1950 he would smack 24 home runs in each season, and in the latter, he also hit .288, by far his best batting average. He would finish the 1949 season with a .243 batting average and 68 RBI.

With Ennis on first and Waitkus on second, Seminick slammed a drive into the left field stands for his second homer of the inning and third of the game. The three-run homer on this at-bat gave him four RBI for the inning.

Hollmig was then hit by a pitch and scored on Jones's triple. Finally, Miller struck out to end the inning.

The Phillies wound up with 10 runs in the inning, six of them unearned, eight hits, one walk, one hit batter, and one error. They went into the ninth with a 12-3 lead. With Rowe still on the mound, he walked Litwhiler, but then retired the side for the next-to-last and 157th win of his 15-year career.

With the onslaught. the Phillies had earned a place in baseball history. Seminick became only the third National League batter to swat two home runs in one inning, and at the time, only the seventh Phillies player to hit three homers in one game.

"I just happened to be swinging where Raffensberger and Peterson were pitching," Seminick said after the game.

No other Phillies team has ever hit five home runs in one inning. The six homers tied the Phillies one-game record, and the 10-run inning matched the second best in club history. Overall, the Phils laced 12 hits in the game, just four more than the Reds.

"It was the best game I've ever seen," said Phils owner Bob Carpenter, who came down to the clubhouse to congratulate his team.

Coincidentally, two games later, in a game against the Giants, Reds pitcher Herm Wehmeier gave up three home runs in succession on four pitches.

The Phillies would go on to win 21 of their 30 games in June, but then lost 25 of their next 41 games. Sawyer gave the team a stern clubhouse lecture, and the team went on to win 27 of its next 43 games and finished the season with an 81-73 record. Along the way the Phils played in games that would go 15, 16, and 18 innings. The season, of course, set the stage for the 1950 campaign when the Phils, with mostly the same lineup, won their first pennant since 1915.

Eddie Waitkus – Came Back to Play After Getting Shot (1949-1950)

In the long history of pro sports, there have been only a few athletes who have been shot. When it is even possible, it's hard to imagine something more difficult for a player to come back from.

Eddie Waitkus is one who did. The Phillies first baseman was shot in a hotel room by a deranged woman. The following season, he not only returned to the diamond, but was a key figure as the Phillies captured the National League pennant.

Waitkus's comeback was absolutely remarkable. Shot and nearly killed mid-season in 1949, he returned the following year and played in every game, putting together an amazing season that included a batting average of .284, 182 hits, while leading the team in doubles with 32 and runs scored with 102, and recorded a .993 fielding percentage. Twice that year he went 5-for-5.

To get to that point, Waitkus had already had an unusual life. Born in Cambridge, Massachusetts, he had signed with the Chicago Cubs in 1939 at the age of 18. Afterward, he spent almost three years in the minor leagues, hitting .326 in his first season and .303 the next year. During this time, he also attended Boston College for one year.

Waitkus, who spoke three foreign languages, was called up to the Cubs late in the 1941 season and appeared in 12 games. He then spent the 1942 season with Los Angeles in the Pacific Coast League and hit .336.

After that season, Waitkus joined the Army during World War II. He became a machine gun operator and participated in several major battles in the South Pacific, after which he was awarded four Bronze Stars.

Waitkus spent three years in the military, then rejoined the Cubs in 1946. He hit .304 that season, then followed up with .292 and .295 averages in the next two years. Mysteriously, he was traded after the 1948 season, going to the Phillies with pitcher Hank Borowy for pitchers Dutch Leonard and Monk Dubiel.

"They can't trade the best first baseman in the business," growled former Cubs manager Rogers Hornsby. "But they did."

It was a great trade for the Phillies as Waitkus quickly became one of the major parts of the team's lineup. "We had Dick Sisler at first in 1948, and he wasn't a very good first baseman," Phils manager Eddie Sawyer said. "When we got Eddie, there was no problem anymore."

Waitkus, who was not a power-hitter, batted third and was hitting .306 when the Phillies traveled to Chicago to meet the Cubs. The team stayed at the well-known Edgewater Beach Hotel.

On June 14, after the Phils split two afternoon games at Wrigley Field, Waitkus went out for dinner with former Cubs and now Phillies teammates Bill Nicholson and Russ Meyer. The trio ate and drank before returning to the hotel around 11 PM.

When they got there, a hotel clerk handed Waitkus a note. "Mr. Waitkus. It's extremely important that I see you as soon as possible," it read. "I realize this is a little out of the ordinary, but as I said, it's rather important. Please come soon. I won't take up much of your time."

Signed by a woman who used the pseudonym of a girl who had been a high school classmate of his, Waitkus was told her room number. Urged by his two teammates to find out what she meant, Waitkus went to her room and knocked on the door. A woman opened the door and let him in.

Unlike the name she had signed on the note, her real name was Ruth Ann Steinhagen. She was a 19-year-old typist for a local insurance company, and a devoted fan of the star first baseman.

> Waitkus crossed the room, sat down in a chair, and said, "Well, babe, what's happening?" The girl replied that she had a surprise for him and walked to a closet, where she pulled out a .22 rifle, and shot Waitkus in the chest. Just missing his heart, the bullet passed through a lung and lodged in his back near his spine.

Steinhagen then called the front desk to report the shooting. When rescuers arrived, they found her holding Eddie's hand and cradling his head on her lap.

Immediately, Waitkus was rushed to the hospital. Sent immediately to the operating room, he nearly died twice before the bullet was finally removed.

Meanwhile, Steinhagen was arrested. She said she was in love with her victim, even had a shrine dedicated to him at her home. She didn't want any other woman to have him, and she wanted to be in the limelight by killing a celebrity. She had planned to stab him with a knife, but he walked past her too fast. She wound up using the rifle she had bought for $21 at a pawnshop. She said that she also planned to commit suicide, but lacked the courage to do it.

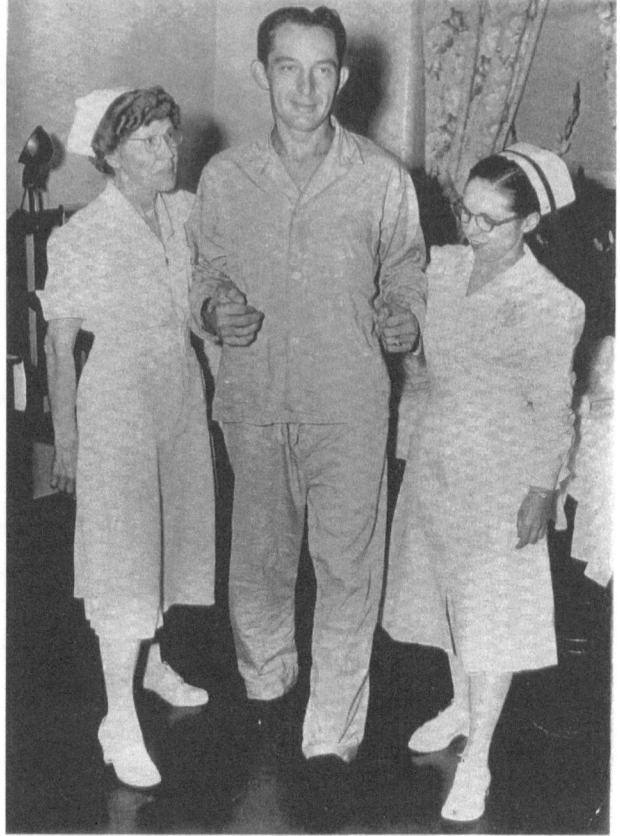

Eddie Waitkus made an amazing comeback after getting shot and nearly killed.

Waitkus was hospitalized for one month. He had four surgeries before returning to Philadelphia on July 17. Meanwhile, Steinhagen was arraigned on a charge of attempted murder. She was indicted by a grand jury, found to be insane, and sent to a mental health institution where she underwent brain therapy.

On August 19, the Phillies held "Eddie Waitkus Night" at Shibe Park. Waitkus was joyously feted and given many gifts. Although he did not play again that season, he finished the year with a .306 batting average in 54 games.

Waitkus spent that winter in Clearwater, Florida, relentlessly working out on a reconditioning program for three months with Phillies trainer Frank Wiechec. Not only did he have a grueling schedule, Waitkus also met a woman who would become his wife.

When spring training began, Waitkus was ready to play. "If it hadn't been for Frank Wiechec," he said, "I don't think I could have been here."

Fortunately, Waitkus went on to have a banner season with the Phillies, as they won only their second pennant in team history. Batting leadoff for much of the season, the player who earned the nickname of "The Fred Astaire of Baseball" because of his stylish physical play, was a major inspiration for his teammates.

"Eddie was a great contact hitter," teammate Richie Ashburn once said. "And as a fielder, he was a magician with the glove." To this, shortstop Granny Hamner added: "We never had to worry about throwing the ball to him. You just let it fly. You knew Eddie would always come up with it." Ashburn also called Eddie "a class guy who was supportive of everybody."

Waitkus's 1950 heroics were highlighted in the final game of the season against the Brooklyn Dodgers when in the 10th inning, he singled and eventually scored the winning run on Sisler's three-run homer that gave the Phillies a 4-1 victory and the pennant. He also caught the final out of the game.

"I'll always remember that game," Waitkus said many years later. "We went as far as we did, and I think it was quite an accomplishment."

Facing the New York Yankees in the World Series, Waitkus hit .267, but the Phillies lost in four games. Later, Waitkus was named by the *Associated Press* as baseball's Comeback Player of the Year.

Waitkus hit just .257 in 1951, but then went on to post a batting average of .289 the next season. In 1953, the Phillies acquired first baseman Earl Torgeson in a deal that relegated Waitkus to a role as a pinch-hitter. When Torgeson was hurt, Waitkus went back to the starting lineup and finished the season with a .291 average.

By then, Waitkus had become the inspiration for a book by Bernard Malamud called *The Natural*. The book was based on a person named Roy Hobbs who was shot by a deranged woman. In 1984, a film called *The Natural* was produced starring Robert Redford.

Waitkus, a two-time All-Star selection, left the Phillies after the 1953 season and joined the Baltimore Orioles. After hitting .259 as a reserve, he returned to the Phils in 1955, hitting .280 in 33 games in what would be the last of 11 big league seasons.

He ended with a career batting average of .285 with 1,214 hits in 1,140 games. He also posted a lifetime fielding percentage of .993 with a meager 73 errors.

Meanwhile, Steinhagen spent just three years in the psychiatric hospital before getting released in 1952. She spent the rest of her life reclusively before her death at age 83.

Richie Ashburn – The Throw That Led to a Pennant (1950)

It is rare for a throw from an outfielder to hold a special place in baseball history. It is just something that typically does not draw wide acclaim when compared with hitting or pitching achievements.

But in the annals of Phillies history, there has been one throw that ranks among the team's greatest feats. It was a throw that paved the way for the Phillies capturing only their second National League pennant and the first one in 35 years.

The throw came on October 1, 1950, in the last game of the season against the Brooklyn Dodgers at Ebbets Field. It was made by 23-year-old center fielder Richie Ashburn. Coming in the bottom of the ninth inning, it erased what would have been the winning run for the Dodgers and enabled the Phillies to win the pennant on Dick Sisler's 10th inning, three-run homer.

The circumstances were virtually unmatchable. The Phillies, known as the Whiz Kids because their roster was filled with young players, were already in the midst of earning a special place in club history.

Over a 31-year period from 1918 through 1948, the Phillies had finished in the first division just once (1932). But after such a devastating streak, it appeared that they were finally escaping that horrendous run when they finished in third place in 1949.

The optimism was well supported. The Phillies had a roster filled with young players, including Ashburn, Del Ennis, Sisler, Granny Hamner, Willie Jones, Mike Goliat, Robin Roberts, Curt Simmons, Bob Miller, and Bubba Church. In addition, they had seasoned players such as Andy Seminick, Eddie Waitkus, Jim Konstanty, Russ Meyer, and Ken Heintzelman

With Eddie Sawyer, a former college professor, serving in his second full year as manager, the Phillies played in a league that included not only Brooklyn, but the New York Giants, Boston Braves, St. Louis Cardinals, and Chicago Cubs, all of whom had or would win pennants between 1945 and 1951. It was truly a tough league.

But the 1950 season changed everything for the Phillies. They would not only replace the Athletics as Philadelphia's favorite team, but they were regarded as an up-and-coming powerhouse that was ready to take its place among the National League's upper class.

A major part of that rise belonged to Ashburn, the Phils' sparkling center fielder, a native of Tilden, Nebraska who was signed for a $3,500 bonus by the Phillies in 1945 as a catcher. While playing on a Phillies farm team in Utica, New York, he had been switched to center field by Sawyer, then that club's manager, because of his dazzling speed.

"He's going to be a great outfielder someday," Phils farm director Joe Reardon rightfully predicted. So great, in fact, that Ashburn, who later spent 35 years as a popular Phillies broadcaster, was voted into the Hall of Fame in 1995.

The left-handed-batting, right-handed-throwing 5-10, 170-pound youngster soon became a standout player. He joined the Phillies in 1948 and quickly became the team's starting center fielder, replacing Harry Walker, the reigning National League batting champion, who failed to report to spring training because he was holding out for a bigger contract.

Richie Ashburn's throw to home nailed what would have been the winning run and cost the Phillies the pennant.

Ashburn went on to win Rookie of the Year honors, hitting .333. It would become the first of eight seasons in his 12 years with the Phillies that Ashburn hit over .300. During that time, he won two batting championships with .338 (1955) and .350 (1958) averages and finished second to Stan Musial twice. He was the last Phillies player to win a batting title.

He also led the league in on-base percentage, singles, and walks four times, and in hits three times (with a high of 221 in 1951). During one stretch of his career, he played in 730 straight games.

A five-time All-Star, his 1,875 hits in the 1950s were the highest number in the majors during that decade. Ashburn currently is first in singles, second in walks, and third in games, at-bats, and hits on the all-time Phillies lists.

> Ashburn was also a masterful defensive player. Six of the 10 highest single-season total putouts by an outfielder belong to Ashburn, including four of the only eight times an outfielder collected 500 or more. Eleven straight seasons his fielding average was .980 or above.

Ashburn ended his 15-year career in 1962. He spent the last three years with the Cubs and New York Mets, finishing with a .308 career batting average. He had 2,574 hits in 2,189 games. With the Phillies, he hit .311 with 2,217 hits, 1,114 runs, and a team record 1,811 singles.

Despite a potent offense that had won many games for the Phillies and had many memorable moments, it was a defensive play that put Ashburn among those who performed the club's all-time greatest feats. It was somewhat ironic, too, because he was not known as someone with a particularly strong throwing arm. In fact, some jokers even called him "Candy Arm."

"He played such a great center field," Seminick once said. "He was such a great outfielder, plus he got on base all the time. He could do it all. And he was always full of enthusiasm. It was fabulous. He had it from the day he came up right to the end."

The Phillies had entered the final game of the 1950 season at the end of a strenuous period. They had popped in and out of first place in the early months of the campaign, then steamed forward to take the lead in late July. By the end of August, they had stretched their lead to nine and one-half games.

The lead dipped to seven games with 11 left to play after a slump in September. The collapse continued, and with two games left in the season, the Phillies had just a two-game lead over the second place Dodgers, who had won 12 of their previous 15 games. Two losses for the Phils would put the two teams into a tie and force a one-game playoff.

That was not a good omen for the exhausted Phillies, who had several key injuries and pitchers too worn out to throw. A 7-3 loss in the next-to-last game put the Phils in a desperate position.

Ironically, the Dodgers had a strong Philadelphia connection. Manager Burt Shotton was the Phils skipper in 1932 when they had their only winning season and first division finish between 1918 and 1949. Third base coach Milt Stock had been the Phillies third baseman when they won their only pennant in 1915. Sisler's Hall of Fame father, George, was the Dodgers' head scout. And catcher Roy Campanella and outfielder Cal Abrams were Philadelphia natives.

The game pitted starters Robin Roberts and Don Newcombe, both looking for their 20th wins. Roberts was exhausted, having started a game two days earlier. This was his fourth start in the last eight games.

Willie Jones singled home Sisler in the sixth inning to give the Phillies a 1-0 lead. Then in the bottom of the sixth, Pee Wee Reese hit a ball into the screen in right field for a home run that tied the score.

The score was still 1-1 as the Dodgers came to bat in the bottom of the ninth. Abrams led off with a walk and reached second on a single by Reese. Duke Snider then slammed a line drive to center field. Already playing shallow, Ashburn roared in and grabbed the ball on one hop.

As he did, Stock, who was fired after the season for what he did, waved Abrams around third with the potential winning run. As Abrams raced home, Ashburn fired the ball to the plate. Catcher

Stan Lopata caught the throw and tagged out the runner 15 feet up the third base line. Roberts then loaded the bases with an intentional walk to Jackie Robinson and got Carl Furillo and Gil Hodges out to finish the ninth and send the game into extra innings.

Ashburn's throw was already being celebrated for saving the Phillies from a grievous defeat. It became even more glorified when Sisler homered to win the game and the pennant.

"To be accurate," Ashburn, who hit .303 that season, said with excessive modesty some years later, "it was a fairly routine play executed perfectly in a very crucial situation."

It was a throw in a game that, climaxed by Sisler's three-run homer in the tenth, will forever be regarded as one of the greatest games in Phillies history. And without that throw, history might have turned out much differently.

Dick Sisler – 10th Inning Home Run Won a Pennant (1950)

On a team led by two future Hall of Famers and a handful of other fine players, it was hard to find a place to play on the 1950 Phillies. But after coming to Philadelphia, Dick Sisler had earned a spot not only as a solid member of the starting lineup, but as one of the club's most popular players.

Sisler was the son of Hall of Famer George Sisler, one of baseball's all-time greatest hitters, who became the top scout of the Brooklyn Dodgers. But Dick would also gain fame in his own right for hitting the biggest home run in Phillies history.

Sisler, who had a brother Dave who pitched in the big leagues, played on a team that was built around young players such as future Hall of Famers Robin Roberts and Richie Ashburn, along with slugger Del Ennis and fiery team captain Granny Hamner.

Sisler joined the Phillies in 1948 in a trade with the St. Louis Cardinals. A rookie in 1946 with the Cardinals, the 6-2, 205-pound native of St. Louis, Missouri played as a reserve his first two years. He became the regular first baseman in his first year with the Phillies, but in 1949 was ticketed for reserve duty when the club acquired first baseman Eddie Waitkus from the Chicago Cubs.

When Waitkus was shot by a deranged girl in a Chicago hotel room in June, Sisler regained his job at first base and wound up the season with a respectable .289 batting average. Then, with Waitkus's return in 1950, the 29-year-old Sisler was sent to left field.

Sisler wound up playing eight years in the big leagues, including four with the Phillies. In a most curious deal after the 1951 season, the Phillies sent him, Andy Seminick, and two others to the Cincinnati Reds for catcher Smoky Burgess, second baseman Connie Ryan, and pitcher Howie Fox. Sisler finished with a career batting average of .276, 55 home runs, and 360 RBI.

Despite a September slump in 1950, the Phillies had a seven-game lead with 11 games left to play. But the losses continued to mount, reducing the Phillies lead to a mere two games, with their last two games coming against none other than the Dodgers. Two wins by Brooklyn would mean a playoff to determine the winner of the National League pennant.

A playoff meant almost certain defeat. The Phils, riddled by injuries and other players being exhausted from excessive use, wanted desperately to win one of the two games to avoid a one-game playoff against the hot Dodgers. When Brooklyn won the opener, 7-3, the stage was set for a tense showdown on October 1, the last day of the season.

Brooklyn was a powerhouse club. Between 1946 and 1956, the team won six pennants and three times lost flags on the last day of the season. Fielding a lineup with future Hall of Famers Jackie Robinson, Pee Wee Reese, Roy Campanella, and Duke Snider, plus standout players such as Carl Furillo and Gil Hodges, the Dodgers, then eight years before moving to Los Angeles, had one of the great teams of all time.

With several thousand Phillies fans making the trip to Brooklyn and a crowd of 35,073 jammed into tiny Ebbets Field—an estimated 30,000 more were turned away at the gate—Roberts, pitching on just two days rest, took the mound for the Whiz Kids against Don Newcombe. Each was going for his 20th win of the season.

The Phillies grabbed a 1-0 lead in the top of the sixth when Sisler singled. After a single by Ennis, he scampered home on a single by Willie Jones. Brooklyn came right back to tie in the bottom half of the inning on a Reese home run.

The greatest home run in Phillies history came off the bat of Dick Sisler.

The 1-1 score was still standing in the bottom of the ninth. Cal Abrams led off for the Dodgers with a walk and moved to second on a single by Reese. Snider then drilled a liner to center. Ashburn fired the ball to the plate and Abrams was out. Roberts then worked his way out of the inning unscored upon.

The weary Roberts led off the 10th with a single. Waitkus followed with another single. Then Ashburn tried to sacrifice, but Roberts was thrown out at third, getting a painful dose of lime in his eye as he slid.

Next up was Sisler, who already had three singles in the game, despite a heavily taped and badly sprained wrist that had kept him out of action three weeks earlier and had been aggravated sliding into second in the fourth inning.

Sisler, however, usually fared well against Newcombe. "I had pretty good luck against him," recalled Sisler, who hit .329 that year against Dodgers pitching. "He was a fastball pitcher, and I was a fastball hitter. I remember the situation vividly."

The fireballing Newcombe got two quick strikes, then wasted a ball. Then he threw one he would forever regret.

"It was a fastball over the plate, high and away," Sisler said. "I swung hard, just hoping I could make contact. The ball sailed out to left field. I didn't think it would go out, so I began running. As I rounded first, I saw it was a home run."

> The ball cleared the left field wall with plenty of room to spare, giving Sisler his 13th home run of the season. His father George watched with mixed emotions from the stands, finally happily tossing his hat in the air as Sisler romped quickly around the bases, arriving at the plate to be engulfed by a mob of ecstatic Whiz Kids.

"As I circled the bases, I thought that would be enough for Roberts because he was tough that day," Sisler said. "He was dead tired, but he was able to dig down and come up with a little extra."

Sisler's blast gave the Phillies a 4-1 lead. Then Roberts, pitching one of the grittiest performances of his life, retired the Dodgers in order in the bottom of the 10th, assuring the Phillies only their second pennant in club history.

"I've hit some better, but none ever meant so much," said Sisler amid the pandemonium of the Phillies locker room. "It's the biggest hit I ever got."

Even the Dodgers thought it was a big hit. Led by Robinson, many of them, including manager Shotton, came across to the Whiz Kids clubhouse to congratulate the team that had just won its first pennant in 35 years.

As soon as the game ended, the celebration began back in Philadelphia. Jubilant Phillies fans spilled into the streets. Car horns honked. Church bells rang. Fire sirens blared. Impromptu parades began as Philadelphians launched a wild party that extended far into the night.

When the Phillies' train arrived in Philadelphia a few hours after the end of the game, an estimated 30,000 fans mobbed the station, hoping to get a glimpse of the players.

"If I hadn't (hit the home run), I don't think people would have remembered me," Sisler said many years later. "I was just another ball player, maybe a little bit better than average."

For sure, they remembered him then. The next morning, in front of Sisler's house in Northeast Philadelphia, stood a mob of fans. One had even hung a sign that said, "We Love You."

The Phillies lost in the World Series to the New York Yankees, four games to none. But for Sisler, who ended the season with a .296 batting average to go with 13 home runs, his name had become a household word in Philadelphia. He would forever be remembered as the man who slammed the biggest home run in Phillies history.

Jim Konstanty – The First Reliever to Win an MVP (1950)

Given the fact that at one time there was no such thing as a full-time relief pitcher, it can certainly be said that no position in baseball has undergone more changes than relief pitcher.

Throughout its early years and into the first half of the 20th century, there was no such thing as a full-time reliever. If a team needed relief, it used one of the starters who was on an off day. Then full-time relief pitchers entered the picture, and they were used for as long and as often as needed. Eventually, the job evolved to the current situation, where relief pitchers clutter a roster, often many are used in a game, and seldom work more than one inning.

Jim Konstanty was one of the pioneers of the art of relief pitching. Not only was he one of the leaders who led the way into creating full-time relief pitchers, he helped to make the job an important and necessary part of the roster.

Konstanty did this during a stint with the Phillies, highlighted in 1950 when he had one of the greatest seasons of any relief pitcher in the baseball history. It was a season that culminated with his becoming the first relief pitcher ever to win a Most Valuable Player Award.

In 1950, relief pitcher Jim Konstanty recorded 16 wins and 22 saves and was the first reliever to win the Most Valuable Player Award.

Being a full-time relief pitcher was never really a part of the game until Fred Marberry of the Washington Senators began coming out of the bullpen during games in the mid-1920s. Although he sometimes started games, Marberry's value was as a talented reliever. It came during a career that extended into the mid-1930s.

Few others, though, followed Marberry's example until the 1940s when the headline relievers were Joe Page of the New York Yankees and Hugh Casey of the Brooklyn Dodgers. Then came Konstanty.

Born in upstate New York in a town ironically named Strykersville, the 6-1, 202-pounder attended Syracuse University, earning a degree in physical education while winning letters in baseball, basketball, soccer, and boxing. Originally a third baseman who switched to first base, he tried out for two minor league teams, but was turned down. So he enrolled in graduate school, played some pro basketball in Utica, and took a job as a high school teacher.

In 1939, Konstanty signed a minor league contract as an infielder. But after showing talent while pitching batting practice, he became a full-time hurler and pitched in the minors, one season losing 19 games, until he signed in 1944 with the Cincinnati Reds.

He posted a 6-4 record, mostly as a starter for the Reds, then spent 1945 in the Navy, and was eventually traded to the Boston Braves. He was sent down to Toronto after 10 games, and was still playing there in 1948 when the Phillies took over the team and sent Eddie Sawyer there as manager.

Late that season, Konstanty, by then 31-years-old, was called up to the Phillies. Sawyer, by then having been moved up to Phillies manager, converted the bespectacled right-hander into a full-time reliever, and in 1949, he worked in 53 games out of the bullpen, posting a 9-5 record with 12 saves.

When in the minors, Konstanty had met an undertaker named Andy Skinner. He was not a player, but he had considerable knowledge about the art of pitching, and after he and Konstanty became friends, he served as Jim's analyst throughout the rest of his days on the mound.

Skinner's help never had a stronger impact than in 1950. It was not only the year the Phillies won their first National League pennant in 35 years. It was a year when Konstanty performed like no reliever before him ever had.

Never one who threw hard, Konstanty's two main pitches were a hard-breaking slider and a palm ball. Taciturn, yet full of energy, he also threw a curve and a changeup. And he always tried to make the batter hit his best pitch.

"That's the reason Jim's so successful," Sawyer once said. "He never deliberately throws a 'sucker' pitch, trying to keep the batter off stride. He tries to make every batter hit into the dirt or pop up."

On a staff that included standout young starters Robin Roberts and Curt Simmons, veterans Russ Meyer and Ken Heintzelman, and rookies Bob Miller and Bubba Church, Konstanty proved to be just what was needed — a reliever who could save games.

At one point, he worked nine innings in a 15-inning, 9-7 win over the Pittsburgh Pirates. Chosen for the National League All-Star team, he pitched a scoreless inning in the NL's 4-3 victory in 14 innings. Then on September 15, Konstanty had a performance like no reliever has ever had before or since.

The Phillies met the Reds in a twi-night doubleheader at Shibe Park. Andy Seminick's home run gave the Phillies a 2-1 victory in the first game. Then Roberts got the start in the second game, but the Phillies fell behind, 5-0, after five innings.

Roberts was replaced by Jack Brittin in the eighth. Then Konstanty entered the game in the ninth. Meanwhile, the Phillies hammered away, and in the bottom of the ninth Granny Hamner's two-run double tied the score at 5-5.

The game went 19 innings with each team scoring two runs in the 18th before the Phillies eked out an 8-7 win on Del Ennis's RBI single.

Konstanty wound up pitching 10 innings before yielding to Blix Donnelly in the 19th. Konstanty allowed six hits, two runs, struck out three, and walked six.

The game, played before a crowd of 20,673, took four hours and 42 minutes, ending at 12:59 AM just 60 seconds before the curfew. The Phillies had 23 hits and left 23 men on base, while the Reds had 15 hits and 17 LOB.

Konstanty went on to finish the season with an amazing 16-7 record with 22 saves in a then-record 74 games. He finished 62 of those games and over one 32-day period pitched in 13 games, allowing just seven hits and no runs in 22.1 innings. While recording a 2.66 ERA, he allowed 108 hits in 152 innings, striking out 56 and walking 50. In all, he had a direct hand in 38 of the Phillies 91 victories.

Konstanty, though, was not done with his stunning appearances. The Phillies fought back from a late September collapse to win the pennant on the last day of the season. Then, with injuries, Simmons departure for the National Guard, and Roberts exhausted from making three starts in the last five games, Sawyer astoundingly named Konstanty as the starting pitcher in the opening game of the World Series against the New York Yankees.

The result was another amazing feat by the energetic fireman. He went eight strong innings, allowing just four hits. A double by Bobby Brown and fly balls by Hank Bauer and Jerry Coleman gave the Yankees one run in the fourth inning, and that was all they needed to give a 1-0 victory to Vic Raschi, who went the distance yielding two hits.

"Brown hit a bad ball," Konstanty said. "I threw him a slider that was at least half a foot outside. But he fell away and just managed to slice it down the left field line."

The Phillies wound up losing the Series in four games. Konstanty pitched in relief in two other games, working a total of 15 innings in the Series while allowing just nine hits and four runs.

> Afterward, Joe DiMaggio praised Konstanty. "He's a great pitcher," the Yankees slugger said. "He showed better breaking stuff than I ever saw. We have no one like him in the American League."

After the season, Konstanty was named the league's MVP, getting 286 points. Stan Musial, already a three-time MVP, placed second with 158 points. A relief pitcher didn't capture an MVP award again until Rollie Fingers won it for the Brewers in the American League in 1981. It was also the first time a Phillies player had won an MVP award since Chuck Klein did it in 1932.

For Konstanty, winning the award was a glittering climax to an amazing season.

Posting a career 66-48 record with 76 saves and a 3.46 ERA in 433 games, he would pitch all or parts of 11 seasons in the majors. Leaving the Phillies in 1954 after compiling a 51-39 record, he was a hurler for the Yankees and then the St. Louis Cardinals before retiring in 1956. Konstanty's record-setting 1950 season set the standard for relief workhorses that few in baseball history before or after him ever matched.

Robin Roberts – Hurled 28 Straight Complete Games (1952-1953)

Down through the years, the word "consecutive" has played an important role as applied to things done on a baseball field. Whether it refers to a positive or a negative, the word usually relates to a streak that goes beyond the normal length.

A look at the records of Robin Roberts reveals that there are many uses of the word consecutive. Together, they help to tell the story of one of baseball's greatest pitchers.

For instance, Roberts won 20 or more games six consecutive years, an accomplishment matched or exceeded in the National League only by Christy Mathewson and Mordecai Brown in the early 1900s. He led the team in innings pitched 11 consecutive times, exceeding 300 innings six straight times. He led the National League in complete games five consecutive years.

Truly, Roberts has a strong hold on the word "consecutive." And he also had a hold on the number 28. Roberts set a career high in 1952 with 28 wins. At one point that year, he also started a streak in which he completed 28 straight games.

No Phillies pitcher has recorded those numbers since Roberts did. And since the pitching mound was moved back to 60-feet, six-inches from home plate in 1893, only four times has a Phillies hurler won more than 28 games in one season, and each time it was Grover Cleveland Alexander who did it.

Speaking of Alexander, Roberts ranks with him and Steve Carlton as the greatest pitchers in Phillies history. It is a trio that dominates the team's statistics for starting pitchers.

Roberts is the Phillies all-time leader in most games (529) pitched. He also leads in complete games (272), and innings pitched (3,739.1), ranks second in wins (234), strikeouts (1,871), and games started (472), and is third in shutouts (35).

On the downside, he also leads the team in losses (199), hits allowed (3,661), runs (1,591), and earned runs (1,437) allowed.

Those last figures notwithstanding, Roberts record with the Phillies is very special. Achieved during 14 seasons with the Phils, it is what earned a place in the Hall of Fame for him in 1976 .

"It was a breeze catching him," said Phillies backstop Andy Seminick. "All you had to do was put your finger down, and he would throw it right there. You didn't have to move at all. His control was just exceptional."

Overall, during 19 years in the big leagues, Roberts posted a 286-245 record with a 3.41 earned run average. In 676 games, he worked 4,688.2 innings, striking our 2,357, walking just 902, and registering 45 shutouts. He also collected 25 saves.

Roberts, who worked with a stunning fastball to go with his pinpoint control, was named to seven All-Star teams, and was the starting pitcher in five of them. He was named Major League Pitcher of the Year in 1952 and 1955 by *The Sporting News*. And he hurled four one-hitters.

Cy Young showing Robin Roberts how he threw one of his pitches.

"Robbie was one of the greatest pitchers of all time," said Eddie Sawyer, the Phillies manager during part of Roberts career with the team. "He could throw a strike anytime he wanted. He wanted to pitch every day. And he never complained."

The 6-foot-1-inch 190-pound right-hander came out of Springfield, Illinois, and after serving in the Army, earned a basketball scholarship to Michigan State University. He played baseball, too, and while pitching in a summer league for two years in New England, he attracted the attention of the Phillies and signed a bonus contract for $25,000.

Assigned to the club's farm team in Wilmington, Delaware in 1948, he spent only two months there, posting a 9-1 record, before getting called up to the Phillies in June. Just 21 years old, he immediately became a starting pitcher. He had a 7-9 record that season but showed great potential.

That potential materialized in the following years as Roberts, called The Springfield Rifle, went to the top of the Phillies rotation. Then in 1950, he had his first sensational year.

By then, the Phillies were known as the Whiz Kids. After finishing in the first division just once in the 31 years between 1918 and 1948, the Phils had begun an upward climb. They finished third in 1949. In 1950, they held the league lead through much of the season.

After a September collapse, they came back to win the pennant on the last day of the season with Roberts getting the win when Dick Sisler hit a three-run homer in the 10th inning to give the Phils a 4-1 victory. Roberts pitched all 10 innings, giving up just five hits, to finish the season with a 20-11 record.

Having started three of the last five games, Roberts was too exhausted to work the World Series opener against the Yankees. He pitched Game Two but gave up a home run to Joe DiMaggio in the 10th inning, and the Phillies lost, 2-1. The Phils lost the Series in four games.

> But Roberts was reaching the top of his game. After recording a 21-15 mark in 1951, he had his greatest season in 1952 when he posted a 28-7 record while leading the league in wins, games started (37), complete games (30), innings pitched (330), and hits (292). Roberts' wins were the most in the National League since Dizzy Dean won 28 in 1935.

He lost the opening game of the '52 season, 5-3 to Sal Maglie and the New York Giants, then won seven consecutive games, including a 10-inning, complete game 4-3 win over the Boston Braves. Roberts then lost four straight games.

His streak of 28 consecutive complete games began in August with a 3-1 win over the Cincinnati Reds and Ewell Blackwell. Then in early September, he did the unthinkable by pitching the entire 17 innings in a 7-6 victory over the Braves in a game won by a Del Ennis home run. Roberts gave up 18 hits while striking out just five and walking three.

Roberts ended the 1952 season with eight consecutive complete games, for a season total of 30. He continued his streak in 1953 on his way to posting a 23-16 record. Along the way, Roberts fired five shutouts. One was a 2-0 victory over the Pittsburgh Pirates in which he pitched the whole 10 innings.

During the season, Roberts posted 20 consecutive complete games to run his streak to 28. The streak finally ended in July. When the season was over, he had set a career-high 33 complete games.

The number 28 had again earned a special place in Roberts' record. And it was still at the top of the Phillies list nearly seven decades later, although it was not a major league record. Jack Taylor of the Cardinals set the record with 39 complete games in the deadball era in 1904.

"In those days, you just went out there and pitched," Roberts said. "You started the game, and just kept going. I never wanted to be taken out. I always wanted to pitch the whole game. I never considered coming out until the manager took the ball away from me.

"I had good strength, and I stayed in shape," he added. "I didn't get tired much. Along with that, I had a good, easy delivery, and I had pretty good stuff."

After the 1953 season, Roberts continued his sparkling pitching. He tossed two one-hitters in 1954. And at one point during the season, Roberts won three games in six days, two of the wins coming in relief.

In 1955, he posted his third consecutive 23-win season. That year, he hurled all 15 innings and scored the winning run in a 3-2 victory over the Cardinals. And in a game against the Giants, he pitched a no-hitter for eight and one-third innings before yielding a home run to Alvin Dark in a 4-2 Phillies win.

"Roberts was as competitive a pitcher as I ever faced," Stan Musial once said. "He didn't waste a lot of motion or argue with umpires. He just stood out on the mound and tried to get you out with his best stuff."

In the years that followed, arm problems began taking a toll, and Roberts' effectiveness began to slip. It didn't help that the Phillies weren't playing very well, having fallen into the second division starting in 1956.

In the fall of 1961, the Phillies sold Roberts to the Yankees for $25,000. But he never pitched for them, getting released at the start of the 1962 season. He then joined the Orioles and had three good years before going to the Houston Astros and then Chicago Cubs, before finishing his career in 1966.

It was a career that had been greatly embellished by the word "consecutive" and the number "28."

Gene Conley – Played Two Pro Sports Simultaneously (1959-1960)

It is certainly not uncommon for a major league baseball player to have performed more than one sport during his younger days. As well-coordinated and athletic as baseball players are, that's to be expected.

Rare, however, is the baseball player who participates as a professional in more than one sport. For many reasons, that is extremely difficult.

Even more rare is the athlete who plays two professional sports simultaneously. That is a virtual impossibility.

But it did happen with Gene Conley. Not only did he play major league baseball, he also played major league basketball. And when it did it, his duties often overlapped.

Of particular significance, the 6-8 Conley played with the Phillies and the Boston Celtics at the same time. How's that for mixed loyalties?

He did it with the Phillies for two seasons between 1958 and 1961. Overall, Conley spent 11 years as an MLB pitcher from 1952 through

1963 and six seasons as an NBA forward from 1952 through 1964 with five years off in-between those basketball campaigns.

Only 12 other athletes have played professionally in baseball and basketball. Five of them played with the Phillies. They are Howie Schultz, Frank Baumholtz, Conley, Dick Groat, and Ron Reed. Among that group, only Schultz played both sports professionally at the same time.

Conley is one of only two athletes who have played for championship teams in two major sports. The other is Hall-of-Fame quarterback Otto Graham, who played for winners in both basketball and football.

Conley played with the Milwaukee Braves when they won the World Series in 1957 and with the Boston Celtics who won three titles from 1959 through 1961. Conley spent parts of those two NBA championship seasons with the Phillies.

Born in Muskogee, Oklahoma, Conley's family moved to Richland, Washington when he was a youth. There, Conley was a three-sport star in high school. He was named to the all-state teams in baseball and basketball and won the state championship in the high jump in track and field.

Conley attended Washington State University where he twice earned honorable mention to the All-American team in basketball and played in the College World Series in baseball.

After being courted by scouts from both sports, Conley signed in 1950 with the Boston Braves. He played in the minors for parts of three seasons, twice being named Minor League Player of the Year while posting 20-9 and 23-9 records at Hartford and Toledo, respectively. He joined the Braves briefly in 1952. That year, he also signed with the Celtics.

After returning from the minors in 1954, Conley played with the Milwaukee Braves for five years. After failing to report to spring training on time in 1959 because the Celtics were in the playoffs,

Conley was traded to the Phillies along with Joe Koppe and Harry Hanebrink for Stan Lopata, Ted Kazanski, and Johnny O'Brien, also a former college basketball star.

The big right-hander finished his career with a 91-96 record, and a 3.82 earned run average in 276 games. In 1,588.2 innings pitched, he allowed 1,606 hits, struck out 888, and walked 511.

In his two years with the Phillies, the tallest pitcher in club history posted a 20-21 record with a 3.34 ERA in 54 games. He fanned 219, walked 84, and gave up 351 hits in 373.1 innings pitched, while hurling for two last-place teams.

Gene Conley played pro basketball and pro baseball at the same time.

In the NBA, Conley played with the Celtics during the 1952-53 season and for three more seasons from 1959 through 1961. He also played with the New York Knicks for two seasons from 1962 through 1964.

Playing mostly as a reserve power forward, Conley appeared in 351 NBA games, scoring 2,070 points for a 5.9 per game average. He also averaged 6.3 rebounds per game.

"Gene Conley was a truly remarkable athlete," Celtics coach Red Auerbach once said. "There was never anyone like him. There's no telling how good he would have been if he had elected to stay in one sport or the other."

By the time Conley came to the Phillies, he had hurled in two All-Star games, being the winning pitcher in 1955 and the losing moundsman in 1954. In 1954, after getting called up in June, he had compiled his best record with a 14-9 mark with a 2.82 ERA, along the way beating the sturdy Brooklyn Dodgers five straight times, two of which were shutouts.

But after going 11-7 in 1955, his season ended after he suffered an injured shoulder — now called a torn rotator cuff — while throwing a pitch to Granny Hamner in a game against the Phillies. Even when he arrived in Philadelphia in 1959, his shoulder injury had not fully healed.

After the shoulder injury, Conley said "I was never the same pitcher again. Hurting my shoulder made me not reach the pitching heights I'd been on my way to. At the time, I was probably as good as any right-hander in baseball."

He pitched well with the Phillies, posting a 12-7 record with a 3.00 ERA in 25 games in 1959. He also pitched two innings in one of the two All-Star games held that year. In that game, he struck out Ted Williams. Then he compiled an 8-14 mark and a 3.68 ERA in 29 games in 1960.

Later that season, Conley was hit by a pitch thrown by the Chicago Cubs' Glen Hobbie, and it broke two bones in his pitching hand. Despite the injury, Conley pitched the full nine innings and won, 3-1.

As part of a pitching staff that at various times included Robin Roberts, Art Mahaffey, Chris Short, Jim Owens, and Jack Meyer, Conley had some outstanding games during his time with the Phillies.

In 1959, he pitched a six-hit, 2-0 win over Milwaukee, a four-hit, 2-1 victory over the Los Angeles Dodgers, a seven-hit, 11-0 triumph over the St. Louis Cardinals, and a three-hit, 4-1 verdict over the Chicago Cubs. That year, Conley led the pitching staff with a 3.00 ERA, which ranked the seventh lowest in the National League.

The following season, Conley had more stellar performances. In one game, he surrendered 10 hits, but captured a 2-0 victory over the Pittsburgh Pirates. Then within six days he won three games.

In the first one, Conley pitched an eight-hit, complete game, 5-2 triumph over the Cincinnati Reds. Two days later, he twirled the final two innings in relief to get the win as the Phils beat the Braves in 10 innings, 8-5. Three days after that, he fired a four-hit complete game to best the Pirates, 2-1. Later that season, Conley hurled another complete game four-hitter to beat the Cubs, 2-0.

In both seasons with the Phillies, Conley helped the Celtics, led by Bill Russell, win the NBA championship.

Playing basketball did not sit well with the Phillies. He had always been implored by teams in both sports to quit one and just play the other.

At the end of the 1960 season, new Phillies manager Gene Mauch told Conley: "Quit worrying about basketball. You're paid to play baseball." Phillies owner Bob Carpenter told Conley in a heated discussion: "I don't want you to play basketball anymore."

"I can't do that," Conley said. "I prefer to continue playing both sports." That conversation eventually ended with Conley getting traded to the Red Sox for Frank Sullivan, another towering pitcher who stood at 6-7.

Conley left Philadelphia with good memories, though. "I really enjoyed my two seasons there," he once said. "I enjoyed the city, the people, and my teammates, although we certainly didn't have a great club. It was a fun team," he added, mentioning the names of Roberts, Richie Ashburn, Willie Jones, and Sparky Anderson.

Conley enjoyed thinking back to his games when the Celtics played the Philadelphia Warriors. In one game against the Warriors and Wilt Chamberlain, he scored 28 points. And in the Eastern Division finals in 1960 against the Warriors at Philadelphia's Convention Hall, he recorded 17 points and 17 rebounds in the deciding game won by the Celtics.

Looking back on his two-sport career, Conley said: "I don't know how I did it." Neither did the rest of the sports world. Playing pro baseball and pro basketball, in some years simultaneously, was a feat that hardly seems possible.

Art Mahaffey set a Phillies record for most strikeouts in a nine-inning game.

Art Mahaffey – Struck Out 17 Batters in One Game (1961)

Striking out a lot of batters in one game is not something that happens very often. But when it does happen, it is regarded as a very special achievement and places the pitcher in an exclusive class of prominent hurlers.

Since the pitching mound was moved back to 60-feet, 6-inches from home plate in 1893, only three pitchers by the end of the fifth decade of the 20th century had struck out as many as 17 batters in a nine-inning game. Dizzy Dean did it in 1933, Bob Feller reached that plateau in both 1936 and 1938, and Sandy Koufax joined the strikeout artists in 1959.

That was it. And then along came Art Mahaffey. The 6-1, 185-pound Phillies right-hander joined the group in 1961 when he fanned 17 Chicago Cubs in a 6-0 victory in the second game of a doubleheader at Connie Mack Stadium. Ironically, the first game was also a shutout with Frank Sullivan blanking the Cubs, 1-0. The two wins were the first time the Phillies swept a doubleheader in 10 years.

Mahaffey's gem set a Phillies record that still stands for most strikeouts in a nine-inning game. (Chris Short fanned 18 New York Mets in a 15-inning game in 1965.) The old nine-inning Phillies record was 13, originally set in 1910 by Earl Moore, then equaled by Ray Benge in 1929, Robin Roberts in 1957, and Jack Sanford, also in 1957. For Mahaffey, then only 23 years old, the record came in just his second year with the Phillies.

A native of Cincinnati, Ohio, Mahaffey had been signed out of high school in 1956. He was the first person who played in the Babe Ruth League ever to be signed by a major league team. He then served in the minors until called up by the Phillies in mid-season in 1960. In didn't take long for Mahaffey to make a favorable impression. His dazzling fastball quickly drew the attention of onlookers.

In his big league debut, Mahaffey gave up a hit to the first batter he faced, then picked him off. Later in the season, he had a perfect game into the sixth inning against the San Francisco Giants before giving up a hit to Eddie Bressoud. Mahaffey ended his first season with the Phils with a 7-3 record and a 2.31 ERA in 14 games and placed third in the Rookie of the Year voting.

> In an amazing accomplishment, he is the only pitcher in major league history to pick off the first three batters in a game to reach base against him.

The year 1961 was one of the low points in Phillies history. The team lost a major league record 23 games in a row while finishing in last place with a 47-107 record, 46 games out of first.

About the only bright spot during the season was Mahaffey's pitching. At one point, he fired a one-hitter against the Milwaukee Braves, allowing only a single to the second batter in the first inning. Then, his sizzling performance against the Cubs sent the Phillies to their highest point of the catastrophic season.

The date was April 23. Back in the day when the starting pitchers warmed up before the game on the side of the dugouts , a crowd of 16,027 was in the stands. Although the Cubs would finish in seventh place that year with a 64-90 record, they fielded an impressive lineup that included Ernie Banks, Billy Williams, Ron Santo, Frank Thomas, and former Phillie, Ed Bouchee. Richie Ashburn was one of the reserves.

Mahaffey, once called "a stopper" by the *Philadelphia Inquirer*'s Allen Lewis, was dealing with some physical problems. He had sprained his back while running in the outfield during spring training. Six days later, he was hit in the forearm by a batted ball. He also had hernia problems.

"I never thought about it," he said at the time. "I was just trying to get them out."

And so he did. Throwing mostly blazing fastballs and once in a while chucking a curve or a changeup, he fanned Cub batters with astonishing regularity. Making his second start of the season, he struck out the side in both the second and sixth inning, and four times he whiffed two batters in the same inning. He fanned Banks, Santo, Thomas, and Don Zimmer each three times.

"They had some decent hitters," Mahaffey said. "But I was just blowing them away. I really had it that day."

Mahaffey said he was aware of his strikeout total as the game progressed. "I knew exactly how many I had, but I didn't know what the record was. The most important thing in my head was to throw a shutout. It was always thrilling to throw a shutout."

While the Cubs were swatting the air, fanning 15 times after seven innings, the Phillies were getting on the scoreboard. Johnny Callison drove in one run in the first inning on a sacrifice fly. Pancho Hererra doubled and scored on an error in the second. Callison added a three-run homer in the fifth. And Tony Taylor singled and eventually scored on a single by Tony Gonzalez in the eighth.

In the eighth inning, Ashburn lined out to right field as a pinch-hitter. Then in the top of the ninth, Zimmer struck out, and Bob Will stroked a single. Santo flew out to left and Banks popped out to second to end the game. A standing ovation in the stands greeted Mahaffey as he walked off the mound and headed for a deliriously happy group of teammates in the dugout.

The Phillies wound up with seven hits, while the Cubs got four. Mahaffey, who later became the first Phillies player ever featured on the cover of *Sports Illustrated* magazine, walked one while throwing 146 pitches, only 48 of them balls.

To Phillies manager Gene Mauch, who did not get along well with Mahaffey, the game left an unforgettable mark. "It was the most powerful game I ever saw in my life," he said.

Over the rest of the horrific Phillies season, Mahaffey went on to post an 11-19 record and a 4.11 ERA in 36 games. He struck out 158 in 219.1 innings pitched. The next year, when the Phillies logged a winning record of 81-80, moving up to seventh place in the newly formed 10-team expansion league, he had the best season of his career

He started out by winning his second straight season opener with a 12-4 win over the Houston Colt 45s. Later, he hit a grand slam homer to beat the New York Mets, 9-4, in a game in which he fanned 12 batters. With the leagues holding two All-Star games that year, he pitched in both, although he was the losing pitcher in the second one at Wrigley Field.

In August, he stopped a Phillies eight-game losing streak with a seven-hit, 11-3 victory over the Cardinals.

> Ultimately, he recorded a 19-14 mark with a 3.94 ERA in 41 games. He had 20 complete games, which tied him with Billy O'Dell of the San Francisco Giants for second in the league, two behind Warren Spahn's 22.

Mahaffey spent three more seasons with the Phillies. He once said that he could have done much better, but Mauch had a habit of yanking his pitchers early in a game.

With arm problems starting to take a toll, he fell to a 7-10 mark in 1963 before coming back with a 12-9 record the following year. That, of course, was the year the Phillies blew a six-and-one-half game lead with 12 games left to play in the season.

After the 1965 season, Art was traded to the St. Louis Cardinals in a deal that brought Bill White and Dick Groat to the Phillies. But the deal didn't pan out for Mahaffey, and, although he had posted a 4-0 record in spring training, he retired during the season.

In his seven years in the big leagues, Mahaffey wound up with a 59-64 record while pitching in 185 games, 148 of which he started. He struck out 639 in 999 innings pitched. He compiled a 58-60 record in 173 games with mostly poor Phillies teams.

None of his strikeouts, though, were as memorable as the 17 he recorded in that sparkling game he pitched in 1961. Now, 60 years later, that still stands as one of the Phillies' most decorated pitching performances.

Jim Bunning – The First Perfect Game in Team History (1964)

Rare is the pitcher who throws a perfect game. Since the pitching mound was placed at 60-feet, six-inches from home plate in 1893, there have been only 21 perfect games thrown in major league baseball through 2020.

The 15th perfect game, the first one hurled during the regular season in 42 years (Don Larsen fired a perfect game in the 1956 World Series) and the first one ever registered in the National League, was pitched by the Phillies Jim Bunning in a game played against the New York Mets at Shea Stadium. Ironically, it was Father's Day, and Bunning eventually was the father of nine children.

It was also Bunning's second no-hitter, the first one coming in 1958 while he was with the Detroit Tigers. At the time, Bunning's perfecto with the Phillies made him only the 12th hurler to throw two or more no-hitters.

The no-hitters were certainly the highlights of Bunning's 17 years in the major leagues. And his perfect game was one of the most memorable occasions in Phillies history.

There were, however, other glittering phases of Bunning's career. He was only the second pitcher (Cy Young was the first) in major league history to win 100 games in both the American and National Leagues. He pitched in seven All-Star Games. He won in double figures 13 times. And in 1996, he was inducted into the Baseball Hall of Fame.

During a career in which the 6-3, 190-pound right-hander spent nine years with the Tigers, six years with the Phillies, and brief times with the Pittsburgh Pirates and Los Angeles Dodgers, Bunning posted a 224-184 record and a 3.27 earned run average. In 591 games, he pitched 3,760.1 innings, gave up 3,433 hits, struck out 2,855, and walked 1,000. Over one 11-year period, Bunning made 399 consecutive starts without missing a single call to the mound.

A perfect game hurled by Jim Bunning gained him a special place in history.

Bunning made two stops in Philadelphia. Traded to the Phillies in 1964, he worked four years with the Phils, then was swapped to Pittsburgh in 1968, and returned to Philadelphia for two seasons before retiring after the 1971 campaign. In 226 games with the Phillies, Bunning posted an 89-73 record, which was diminished by two poor seasons at the end, in which he was 15-27 overall.

"The two toughest competitors I ever faced," recalled Pete Rose, "were Jim Bunning and Bob Gibson. He (Bunning) had great stuff, and he was awesome against right-handed hitters."

To that, Phils catcher Bob Boone added: "He had the best control of any pitcher I ever caught. I'd put the glove here, and he'd hit it."

The native of Southgate, Kentucky, was the starting pitcher in the last game at Connie Mack Stadium and the first game at Veterans Stadium.

> A no-nonsense, often feisty, tough-minded competitor, Bunning earned a degree at Xavier University, majoring in economics, then spent nearly six years in the minors before getting a call in 1955 from the Tigers. Then, after dividing time between the minors and Detroit for the next two years, he became a full-time starter in 1957, and posted a 20-8 record while being the starting and winning pitcher in the All-Star Game.

He won in double figures in each of his remaining seven years in Detroit while twice leading the American League in strikeouts with 201 each year.

In 1958, Bunning fired a no-hitter, beating the Boston Red Sox, 3-0, in the first game of a doubleheader at Fenway Park. Bunning struck out 12 and walked two. He retired Ted Williams, in the process of winning his second straight batting title, on a fly ball to Al Kaline in right field for the last out.

Sometime later, Williams said, "It was the most amazing game I've ever been in." His reason was that the Red Sox knew nearly every pitch that was coming because their first base coach, Del Baker, was stealing signs and tipping off the batters. Bunning threw the no-no despite that huge disadvantage.

Bunning was dealt to the Phillies in December 1963, and in his first year, he posted a 19-8 record with a 2.63 ERA. Early in the season, he tossed a one-hitter against the Houston Colt '45s. Then on June 21, before a crowd of 32,026 at Shea Stadium, he fired his perfect game.

"From the beginning, it was obvious that Bunning had his best stuff," wrote former Philadelphia *Inquirer* sports writer Allen Lewis in *Phillies Report*. "He had a darting slider, a tantalizing curve, a good fastball, and almost perfect control."

Bunning got several well-timed defensive plays. In the fifth inning, Jesse Gonder smashed a hot grounder between first and second. Second baseman Tony Taylor dove for the ball and gloved it, but the ball popped out of his glove when he hit the ground. Taylor retrieved the ball and threw from his knees to get the batter out at first.

"It was a great play," Bunning said after the game. "When he did that, I knew I had something special going on."

In the sixth, another crucial defensive play happened when Johnny Briggs raced back to deep center on a fly ball by Charlie Smith and made the catch right in front of the fence.

Meanwhile, the Phillies scored one run in the first inning on rookie Richie Allen's single, and another run in the second on a double by Gus Triandos. Then, a four-run sixth featuring Johnny Callison's home run, an RBI single by Triandos, and a two-run double by Bunning gave the Phillies a 6-0 lead, which turned out to be the final score.

By the ninth inning, Mets fans were cheering Bunning on every pitch. He got Smith to pop out to shortstop Bobby Wine, then struck out pinch-hitters George Altman and John Stephenson, who fanned on a 2-2 curve ball to end the game, played in two hours and 19 minutes.

Bunning finished with 10 strikeouts. He threw just 90 pitches, 69 for strikes. The win gave him a 7-2 record. To complete the memorable day, 18-year-old rookie, Rick Wise, beat the Mets in the second game of the doubleheader, 8-2, in his first major league start.

The masterful hurler would go on to record a 19-8 record that season while posting a 2.63 ERA in 284.1 innings. Despite Bunning's brilliant pitching, though, the Phillies, who were stationed in first place through much of the second half of the season, lost 10 games in a row at the end of the season and blew a 6 1/2 game lead in a staggering collapse that cost them the pennant.

Bunning, however, went on to post 19 wins in three straight years, working 314 innings one season and averaging more than 300 innings during those three years. He won 17 in 1967, while leading the league in innings pitched (302.1), strikeouts (253), shutouts (six), and games started (40).

That year, throwing for a weak team, he encountered numerous instances of hard luck, losing five games by 1-0 scores. He also won three games by 1-0 scores. "That happens," Bunning said.

Widely respected by virtually all who came up against him, Bunning once drew the praise of former player and manager Don Zimmer. "You can't be a more fierce competitor than Bunning was," he said. "I always respected him as a pitcher, even though he had a little meanness in him."

So highly regarded was Bunning that he was usually matched against top pitchers. He regularly faced such moundsmen as Bob Gibson, Sandy Koufax, Juan Marichal, Ferguson Jenkins, Gaylord Perry, and Jim Maloney in National League games.

After the 1967 season, the Phillies traded Bunning to Pittsburgh where he played for nearly two years before getting sent to the Dodgers, who released him at the end of the 1969 campaign. Bunning, whose highest salary was $75,000, was signed as a free agent by the Phillies.

Now on a downhill slide and pitching for bad teams, Bunning had two poor seasons with the Phillies. But in 1970, he did win his 100th National League game when he defeated the Houston Astros, 6-5, in what was his fourth attempt to reach that pedestal.

Later that year, before a raucous season-high 31,822 fans, he beat the Montreal Expos, then managed by Gene Mauch, 4-1, in the last game played in the 62-year history of Shibe Park/Connie Mack Stadium. The following spring, he again beat the Expos, 4-1, in the first game at Veterans Stadium.

Bunning, who would later become a United States Congressman and Senator, retired after the 1971 season. His perfect game seven years earlier would be remembered as one of the greatest pitching performances in Phillies history.

Johnny Callison – Hit All-Star Game's Greatest Home Run (1964)

There have been many noteworthy home runs hit in All-Star games. Some even played a significant role in the outcome of a game.

But there was never a more dramatic home run hit in an All-Star game than the one smashed by Johnny Callison in 1964. Callison's homer holds a place at the top of the list among the greatest four-baggers ever hit in the mid-summer classic.

The homer, coming in the bottom of the ninth inning, won the game for the National League. And it earned for Callison a special spot in Phillies history.

Callison was no stranger to the spotlight. A sweet-swinging right fielder, he was one of the key players in the Phillies lineup during the 1960s and was in the midst of an outstanding six-year run when he hit the majestic home run.

The 5-10, 175-pound native of Qualls, Oklahoma, had come to the Phillies in 1960 in a controversial trade with the Chicago White Sox for pinch-hitting standout, Gene Freese. At the time, Callison had played parts of two inconsequential seasons in Chicago, and with the popular Freese sent away, fans were not happy.

> "I was playing in Venezuela," Callison remembered. "I saw my picture and Freese's in the paper. The writing was in Spanish, so I had to find somebody to translate it for me. That's when I learned I'd been traded. But I was really disappointed. I was going from a first-place club to a last-place club."

Originally signed in 1957 out of high school in California, where he had lived for 12 years, Callison played parts of three seasons in the minors. In his first year, he hit .340 with 17 home runs at Bakersfield in the Class C California League. Then with the Triple-A Indianapolis Indians in the American Association, he led the league in home runs with 29. It was enough for opposing manager Gene Mauch of Minneapolis to say that the youngster "has batting power like Mel Ott."

At one point during his minor league days, Callison and his family survived a major accident near Cheyenne, Wyoming, when their car hit a truck and rolled down an embankment, turning over three times. Amazingly, nobody was seriously injured.

Callison spent parts of the 1958 and 1959 seasons with the White Sox. In his first big league game, the then-19-year-old left-handed swinger went three-for-three. But after hitting .173 in 49 games in 1959, the White Sox unloaded him that December. And a star was born.

In his first two years with the Phillies, Callison hit just .260 and .266 with nine homers each season. But then he blossomed in 1962 with a

.300 batting average, 23 homers, and 83 RBI. He followed that with a .284-26-78 season in 1963.

Then the 1964 season arrived. For many reasons, it was a year that ranks as one of the most unforgettable in the annals of Phillies baseball.

It was the year when Jim Bunning hurled the first perfect game ever thrown by a Phillies pitcher. It was also the year that a hard-hitting young player then named Richie Allen made his Phillies debut. And it was a year when the Phillies fell apart at the end of the season, suffering a mind-boggling collapse that lost a pennant that they surely had just about won.

Callison, though, was one of the brightest spots for the team that season. He hit .274 with 31 home runs, 104 RBI, and 101 runs. But it was a midseason game that placed his name in the history books.

The date was July 7. The place was Shea Stadium in New York, just three months after the ballpark opened. The National League met the American League in the 34th All-Star Game.

Both teams were loaded with superstars. The National League had Willie Mays, Roberto Clemente, Hank Aaron, Billy Williams, and Orlando Cepeda. The American League roster included Mickey Mantle, Brooks Robinson, Harmon Killebrew, Tony Oliva, and Jim Fregosi.

Some 50,850 fans were in the seats for the game. The Nationals had an early lead with the help of solo homers by Williams and Ken Boyer in the fourth inning. Then a two-run triple by Robinson in the sixth off Callison's teammate Chris Short tied the score at 3-3.

In one of many Phillies connections in the game, future manager Fregosi sent the Americans ahead 4-3, with a sacrifice fly in the seventh. The score stood at that until the bottom of the ninth.

With Dick Radatz now pitching in his third inning for the visitors, Mays led off with a single. He then stole second and scored the tying run when Cepeda singled and AL first baseman Joe Pepitone made a wide throw to the plate. Boyer was up next, and he popped out. Johnny Edwards was given an intentional walk. Aaron, who was sick and couldn't start, struck out as a pinch-hitter.

It was now Callison's turn to bat. Johnny had come off the bench as a pinch-hitter for Bunning and popped out to shortstop in the fifth inning, and then was out on a fly to deep center field in the seventh. This time it was the ninth inning with two outs and Curt Flood, pinch-running for Cepada, on second, and Edwards on first.

Callison swung on the first pitch and crushed the ball to deep right field. Up and up it went, finally landing deep in the seats. Three runs scored, and the National League had a 7-4 victory. The win would bring the National League to a 17-17 tie in the All-Star games, the first time it had reached that level in the history of the game.

Jubilation abounds on the National League side after Johnny Callison's walk-off homer in the 1964 All-Star game.

"The pitch was up and tight," Callison remembered years later. "I got around on it. I was using Billy Williams' bat, which was lighter than mine. I was looking for a fastball because that's all he threw. If he'd have thrown me an off-speed pitch, I probably would've fallen on my face."

For Callison, his heroic walk-off home run would stand thereafter as one of the most memorable feats in All-Star Game history. It would also be the first home run in the midsummer classic ever slugged by a Phillies batter, preceding ones by Allen (1967), Greg Luzinski (1977), and Mike Schmidt (1981).

Of course, Callison was named the game's Most Valuable Player, the first and only one for the Phillies. And for the rest of his life, the clout would make him a very special attraction wherever he went.

"That game was unquestionably the biggest thrill of my life," Callison recalled. "I didn't really expect to play much. I figured I'd pinch-hit. But Aaron got sick, so I got in the game."

Unfortunately, that season the Phillies, who for much of the year looked like a certain pennant winner, went on to blow a 6 ½ game lead with 12 games to play, dropping 10 in a row to knock themselves out in a classic collapse.

And Callison, who finished second to Boyer in the NL voting for Most Valuable Player, and Mauch, the Phillies manager since 1960, repeatedly battled in what Johnny recalled "was pure Hell." But, he added, "I'll tell you one thing. Basically, he was the best manager I ever played for as far as baseball strategy goes."

In 1965, Callison, who that year would become a three-time All-Star Game selection, hit .262 with 32 home runs, and 101 RBI. But after four standout seasons, he started to drift downward, and his final four seasons with the Phillies were far short of what he'd done. One exception came in 1968 when he achieved the rare feat of playing the entire season without making an error.

Johnny was traded to the Chicago Cubs after the 1969 season. Then after two more mediocre seasons he was sold to the New York Yankees where after an injury-riddled two years, he retired after the 1973 season.

Callison wound up with a career batting average of .264 with 1,757 hits, 226 home runs, 840 RBI and 926 runs in 1,886 games. With the Phillies over a 10-year period, he hit .271 with 1,432 hits, 185 home runs, and 666 RBI in 1,438 games. And possessing what was called a "cannonball arm," he registered 159 assists with the Phils and 175 altogether.

Even now, although Callision is typically rated as one of the finest Phillies all-around players and was a real favorite of the fans, he is most frequently remembered for his All-Star Game home run. Nobody else has ever hit one with the same dramatic results as Callison.

Over a period of 21 games, Dick Allen compiled an off-the-charts batting record. (Photo courtesy of Bob Bartosz.)

Dick Allen – A Hitting Binge Like Few Ever Had (1966)

Usually, when a player has a sparkling hot streak, his name goes into the headlines and he is long remembered for what he did. It is especially the case when the player already has a noteworthy set of credentials.

That was certainly the case with Dick Allen. During a career in which he earned a place as one of the Phillies foremost hitters, Allen did many special things with his bat. One was among the rarest of its kind in Phillies history.

During a 19-day spree in 1966, Allen compiled a batting record that was simply amazing. In 21 games from June 1 through June 18, Allen laced eight home runs, 26 hits, and drove in 27 runs. Twice he collected four RBI in one game.

Allen's career record with the Phillies was equally as impressive. In nearly nine seasons with the Phils he socked 204 home runs, accumulated 655 RBI, and hit .291. Four times he hit over .300, and three times he smacked more than 30 home runs. His .530 slugging percentage ranks second on the Phils all-time list, just behind Chuck Klein.

Many of his homers were tape-measure blasts, one of which flew over the billboard on top of the left field roof at Connie Mack Stadium and landed on the other side of the houses along Somerset Street. The blow was measured to have traveled 529 feet.

Another time, he smoked a ball over the center field wall between the flagpole and the upper deck. No other ball ever left the ballpark at that location.

Despite his notoriety for hitting the long ball, Allen once said: "I like to think there were other things in the game that I could do besides hit the long ball. But people don't see that."

During a 15-year career that including two stints with the Phillies (1963-69 and 1975-76), plus three seasons with the Chicago White Sox and one each with the St. Louis Cardinals, Los Angeles Dodgers, and Oakland Athletics, Allen compiled a lifetime batting average of .292, with 1,848 hits, 351 home runs, 1,119 RBI, and 1,099 runs scored.

With the White Sox, Allen led the American League in home runs twice, and in 1972 was the league's Most Valuable Player after he hit .308 and led the AL with 37 homers and 113 RBI. He hit .316 and .301 in his other two seasons with the Chisox.

"Of all the players I ever played with or against, and that included Willie Mays, Hank Aaron, Mickey Mantle, and Ernie Banks," star first baseman and Allen teammate Bill White recalled, "Dick Allen hit the ball harder than anybody. Even his ground balls to right or left field were hit hard. He was an awesome, awesome player."

Using a 42-ounce bat, the native of Wampum, Pennsylvania was an All-State basketball player who led his team to two state championships. The 5-11, 187-pound slugger was also one of those rare players who had two brothers, Hank and Ron, play in the major leagues.

Signed by Phillies scout Johnny Ogden for a $70,000 bonus in 1960, Allen spent parts of four seasons in the minors before joining the

Phillies late in 1963. Ogden said later that Allen was the only player he ever saw who hit the ball as hard as Babe Ruth.

Playing third base for the first time in his career after performing at shortstop, second base, and in the outfield, Allen was the National League's Rookie of the Year in 1964 when he hit a career high .318 with 29 home runs, 91 RBI while leading the league in runs (125), triples (13), extra-base hits (80), and total bases (352) in what is often regarded as one of the top rookie seasons anybody ever had.

That was the year in which the Phillies staged their infamous collapse by blowing a 6 1/2 game lead with 12 games left in the season despite Allen's .438 batting average during those 12 games.

The next year he was named to the league's All-Star team, one of seven times during his career that he was chosen for that squad.

> "I never enjoyed a player more than I enjoyed Richie (the name he was called in his early days) Allen," manager Gene Mauch once said.

In 1966, Allen had his greatest season. He led the National League in slugging percentage with a .632 mark, plus he hit a career-high 40 home runs, while batting .317 with 110 RBI and 112 runs scored. Allen's home run total, which included three inside-the-park homers, ranked second in the league behind Aaron's 44, his RBI number placed third, and his batting average was fourth.

Amazingly, in late April, Allen, who would go on to finish fourth in the Most Valuable Player voting, injured his shoulder while sliding into second base at Wrigley Field and he did not make the starting lineup again until May 27.

On June 1, Allen hit a double in a Phillies 4-3 win in the first game of a doubleheader against the Chicago Cubs. Then, in the second game, he laced a single and home run and collected four RBI in a 7-4 Phils victory.

The next day, Allen had a homer and two RBI off Ferguson Jenkins in a 5-4 Cubs win. He followed that with his third homer in three games, plus a double, and one RBI in a 6-1 triumph over the San Francisco Giants. He then collected a single and an RBI in another 6-1 win over the Giants before having his first of three 0-for-3 games.

A single, double, home run and two RBI came afterward in a 6-2 verdict over the Giants. Then a single, triple and two RBI led the Phils to a 5-1 victory over the Cincinnati Reds. Another homer and two RBI followed when the Phillies defeated the Reds, 10-6. Allen had hit three homers and drove in eight runs in the last five games.

In the next three games, the man with the nickname of "Crash," was blanked twice in three at-bats. In between, he posted a home run and two RBI in a 5-4 loss to the Cardinals.

On June 12, Allen launched a nine-game hitting streak that included a single in a 5-3 win over the Cardinals, a triple and an RBI in a 6-2 verdict over the Atlanta Braves, a double and two RBI in a 6-4 victory over the Braves, two singles and one RBI in a 11-6 defeat by the Braves, and one single in a 7-6 loss to the Reds.

Then he slugged a home run in a 9-6 loss to the Reds, a single, home run, and four RBI in a 12-5 win over the Reds, and two singles in a 6-5 win over the Cards. On August 18, Dick homered and drove in two runs in a 3-2 loss to St. Louis. The streak ended the next game.

"It was an amazing, amazing streak," White said.

After that game, Allen had four straight hitless games. He then bounced back with hits in four of the next six games. He homered in two of those games, and in one of them slammed a single and double and drove in four in a 7-3 win over the Atlanta Braves.

During Allen's streak, the Phillies won 12 games and lost seven. The Phillies would go on to a fourth-place finish in the 10-team National League.

After three more seasons with the Phillies, Allen, who should be in the Hall of Fame, was traded to the Cardinals. By then, he had become a first baseman, but was still a great hitter.

By the time he finished his career in 1977 with Oakland, Allen had established himself as one of the finest hitters of his era. Topping it off was his sizzling 1966 season when he staged one of baseball's most amazing streaks.

Rick Wise – A No-Hitter and Two Homers in the Same Game (1971)

Throwing a no-hitter isn't something that happens very often. Neither is hitting two home runs in one game. But when the two are done by the same player in the same game, it is an extraordinary event.

It has only happened once in all of baseball history. And it was done by Phillies pitcher Rick Wise in a game against the Cincinnati Reds in 1971.

Before that, only three other major league pitchers — Wes Ferrell in 1931, Jim Tobin in 1944, and Earl Wilson in 1962 — ever hurled a no-hitter and hit a home run in the same game. And only 65 pitchers throughout baseball history ever threw a complete game and hit more than one homer in the same game.

Wise, a 6-1, 190-pound right-hander, came close to firing no-hitters several other times during his career. And during 18 years in the big leagues, he proved to be a better long-distance swatter than most pitchers.

A native of Jackson, Michigan who was raised in Portland, Oregon, Wise was signed by the Phillies right out of high school. He spent less than one year in the minors, then at the age of 18, was called up to the Phillies in June 1964.

In his first big league start, Wise beat the New York Mets, 8-2, in the second game of a doubleheader at Shea Stadium. The day was made famous because Jim Bunning pitched a perfect game for the Phillies in the opener.

Wise went on to post a 5-3 record in his rookie season. He then registered losing seasons in three of the next five years, the exceptions being his 11-11 in 1967 and 15-13 in 1969. No one doubted Wise's ability from the mound. He just played for mediocre to bad teams.

Wise's ability, though, was easily noticeable in 1968 when the Phillies met the Los Angeles Dodgers at Dodger Stadium. He fired a one-hitter to beat LA, 1-0, with Dick Allen's ninth inning home run providing the winning margin. The only hit off Wise was a second inning bouncer by Bart Shirley that took a bad hop off shortstop Roberto Pena's glove. The play could have been scored as an error, but Shirley was rewarded with a hit and Wise's was denied a no-hitter.

Then, despite playing on a team that lost 95 games in 1971, Wise's fortunes changed on June 23 when he faced the Reds at Riverfront Stadium. The Reds were loaded with top-ranked players, including Pete Rose and George Foster and future Hall of Famers Johnny Bench and Tony Perez.

Wise, who was recovering from the flu, took the mound with a 7-4 record. He had 58 career wins and seven home runs coming into the game.

Leading off the first inning, Rose hit a sharp grounder to shortstop Larry Bowa, who made a nice stop and threw him out at first. Wise then retired the next 15 batters. In the third inning, third baseman John Vukovich provided the defensive play of the game when he made a backhanded stop of a blast hit by Tommy Helms, then threw him out at first.

No player has ever duplicated Rick Wise's feat of belting two home runs while pitching a no-hitter.

Center fielder Willie Montanez grabbed a hard line drive by Rose in the fourth inning, and Vukovich made another fine play in the fifth when he threw out Bench at first after snaring a bouncer to deep third.

Meanwhile, the Phillies had taken a 1-0 lead in the second. In the top of the fifth, Roger Freed was on second base with a double when Wise came to bat. Facing Ross Grimsley, Wise blasted a pitch out of the park to give the Phillies a 3-0 advantage.

In the sixth inning, Wise's perfect game ended when he walked Dave Concepcion on a 3-1 pitch. Concepcion was the only Reds batter to reach base in the game.

Wise's bat went to work again in the eighth when he led off the inning with another home run, this one off reliever Clay Carroll. With the blow, Wise set a record that most likely will never be matched.

"I had two home runs going into that game, so I wasn't surprised," recalled Wise. "I always swung the bat pretty well and tried to help myself."

In the bottom of the eighth, Vukovich made another sparkling play when he snared a high-hopper by Perez and threw him out at first. Then in the ninth, Wise retired the first two batters. Rose was the next batter, and Wise got him to line a 3-2 pitch to Vukovich for the final out.

"He was the last hitter you ever want to see," Wise said about Rose coming to the plate in that situation. Winning 4-0, the 25-year-old Wise finished with just three strikeouts. The Reds grounded out 17 times.

"It was certainly the greatest game of my career," said Wise, who was named to his first of two All-Star teams that season. "Any no-hitter against a major league club is quite an accomplishment, but on the road against Cincinnati, it made for a very great night."

It wasn't Wise's only great night at the plate that season. Incredibly, he also belted two home runs in a game on August 28th, making him only the sixth pitcher in history to go deep twice in a game in the same season.

In the second game of a doubleheader against the San Francisco Giants at the new Veterans Stadium, Wise smacked a solo homer in the fifth inning to give the Phillies a 3-2 lead. Then in the seventh, with the score tied, 3-3, Wise came to bat with the bases loaded. Again, he put one over the wall for a grand slam to give the Phillies a 7-3 win. Wise tied a career-high with 11 strikeouts.

But Wise wasn't finished yet. On September 18, in a game against the Chicago Cubs at The Vet, he pitched all 12 innings in a 4-3 victory. At one point he retired 32 Cubs in a row, which ranks second on the all-time list, following Harvey Haddix's 36 straight for the Pittsburgh Pirates in 1959.

Wise gave up only five hits and struck out 10. And, to clinch the victory and add to his fame as a hitter, he drove home the winning run with a single in the bottom of the 12th. It was Wise's third hit of the game.

Wise finished the 1971 season with a 17-14 record, 17 complete games, a 2.88 ERA, a .237 batting average, and a career-high 15 RBI. He also wound up with six home runs on the season, rare territory for a pitcher.

Right before spring training began in 1972, the Phillies made one of the most shocking moves in club history. They traded Wise, their best pitcher, to the Cardinals for pitcher Steve Carlton. According to Tim McCarver, who would be the catcher for both pitchers, it was a good trade for both teams.

As the story goes, both pitchers were having contract disputes with their teams. Finally, with both teams unwilling to negotiate any longer, they made the swap. As it turned out, it became one of the best trades the Phillies ever made, with Carlton going on to a brilliant career that led him to the Hall of Fame.

Wise wound up with a 75-76 record, a 3.60 ERA, and 717 strikeouts in 219 games with the Phillies.

He went on to post 16-16 and 16-12 seasons with the Cardinals. In 1973, he came close to becoming only the second pitcher in history (Addie Joss was the first) to pitch two no-hitters against the same team. Wise tossed a one-hitter against the Reds, allowing only a one-out, ninth-inning single to Joe Morgan.

Wise was swapped to the Boston Red Sox after the 1973 season. In 1974, he lost another bid for a no-hitter when he gave up a two-out, ninth-inning home run to George Scott in a game against the Milwaukee Brewers.

In 1975, Wise, working in relief, was the winning pitcher when Carlton Fisk hit his famous 12th-inning, walk-off home run in the sixth game of the World Series against the Reds. That season, he recorded his career single-season high in victories with 19.

Wise spent four years in Boston, and two each with the Cleveland Indians and San Diego Padres, before retiring after pitching one game in 1982. He finished his career with a 188-181 record and a 3.69 ERA in 506 games. In 3,127 innings, he struck out 1,647 while recording 30 shutouts. He had 15 career home runs, but none as memorable as his two in 1971.

Steve Carlton in 1972 was a classic example of someone winning for a loser.

Steve Carlton – Won 27 of the Team's 59 Victories (1972)

When a team has such a poor season that it wins only 59 games, you know the players on the team couldn't have done very much. A number like that is a sure sign that there were few decent performances.

That is especially true of the pitching staff. If a hurler wins 10 or 12 games on a team with 59 wins, it would be a noteworthy achievement.

The 1972 Phillies were one of those gruesome teams. They stumbled their way to a 59-97 record and a last place finish in a six-team East Division, finishing 37 1/2 games out of first place. Only one other time since 1945 had the Phils won fewer games.

Of all the poor individual performances, though, there was one that was absolutely astounding. Steve Carlton won 27 games (46% of the team's total and a career high), what has to be one of the greatest single-season pitching performances of all time.

Adding to that record, the slender, 6-5, 210-pound left-hander led the National League in wins, earned run average (1.97), innings pitched (346.1), games started (41), complete games (30), strikeouts (310), and hits allowed (257). After the season, he won his first Cy Young Award.

Although he won more than 20 games three more times during a 15-year career with the Phillies, Carlton's performance in 1972—coming while playing on a such a woeful team—is simply unfathomable.

Carlton was in his first season with the Phillies after coming from the St. Louis Cardinals in a controversial trade for pitcher Rick Wise. In five full seasons (plus parts of two others) with the Cards, Carlton had posted a 77-62 record, winning 20 games in 1971, once losing 19, and once striking out 19 batters in a game.

Of course, it was not foreseeable then that Carlton would win four Cy Young Awards and post a career record of 329-244 becoming the second-winningest left-handed pitcher in baseball history (behind Warren Spahn with 363). But still, even at the time, he was considered a much stronger hurler than Wise.

During a 24-year career, his 4,136 strikeouts are also second all-time for a left-hander, behind only Randy Johnson. Winning in double figures 18 years in a row ranks him ninth on baseball's all-time list in that category. Carlton was inducted into the Baseball Hall of Fame in 1994.

Once asked to describe Carlton's greatest assets, catcher Bob Boone reeled off a litany of terms. "Work ethic," he said. "Character. Competitiveness. Physical strength. He had a tremendous heart. A tremendous fastball. A tremendous slider. He had everything a pitcher needed."

A 10-time All-Star, Carlton, who played briefly with the San Francisco Giants, Chicago White Sox, Cleveland Indians, and Minnesota Twins during the last three years of his career, registered a 241-161 mark with the Phillies. That's the most wins in Phils history. He also heads the club's all-time best list in strikeouts (3,031) and games started (499), while placing second in innings pitched (3,697.1) and shutouts (39).

During his time with the Phillies, as well as throughout the rest of his career, Carlton had a huge list of admirers. Trying to hit Carlton's pitches was "like trying to drink coffee with a fork," Pittsburgh Pirates slugger Willie Stargell once said.

Standout hitter George Brett added, "He was one rough pitcher. You couldn't give in. You had to fight. You had to grind it out. I didn't hit against him that often, but when I did, I always knew I was in for a battle."

"Lefty was a craftsman. An artist," Richie Ashburn once said. "He was a perfectionist. He painted a ballgame. Stroke, stroke, stroke. And when he got through, it was a masterpiece."

Carlton's performances on the mound also featured a highly focused mindset. "The mental game," he said, "is the most important part of my approach. I go out there to win every game. I know what I needed to do to succeed."

Carlton was also a physical fitness devotee. When he pitched, he worked out before a game then again for several hours after a game. And when he wasn't pitching, he also worked out before and after games, sometimes for as much as five hours into the wee hours of the morning. He could do 1,100 sit-ups at a time with 15-pound weights wrapped around each wrist and ankle.

"Whoever put that man together genetically did one helluva job," said Phillies strength and conditioning coach and Carlton's closest ally, Gus Hoefling, "I've never seen anything like it."

Indeed, Carlton, who refused to talk to the media during most of his career, was obsessed with every part of his game, and each day presented a special kind of battle.

There was never a bigger battle between Lefty, as he was called, and opposing hitters then during the 1972 season. The Miami, Florida native joined a group of highly mediocre Phils players, including a pitching staff whose next biggest winner would win seven games.

The season started 10 days late because of a labor dispute. When it did begin, Carlton was the opening day pitcher against Ferguson

Jenkins and the Chicago Cubs. Carlton gave up four hits in eight innings with the Phillies winning, 4-2.

In his next game, Carlton fired a three-hitter to beat Bob Gibson and the Cardinals, 1-0. Carlton was even better in his next start when he gave up a leadoff single in the first inning and no hits the rest of the way, striking out 14 and beating Juan Marichal and the Giants, 3-0.

Carlton wound up winning five of his first six starts. But then he fell into a deep pit, losing five straight games. At the end of May, his record stood at 5-6.

He bounced back in June, winning four games during the month. In his first game that month, he downed the Houston Astros, 3-1, to snap a nine-game Phillies losing streak.

The win launched Carlton on a spectacular 15-game winning streak, breaking an all-time Phillies record that had stood since 1886. Five of those games were shutouts and 14 were complete games. Carlton beat every team in the league at least once while working every four days. He also had three no-decision outings.

"I didn't get involved in the momentum of the streak," he told the author many years later. "I didn't worry about what happened yesterday or what was going to happen tomorrow. Before each game, I went over the pitches I normally threw. Then I'd go out and build on that and try not to make many mistakes."

Game after game Carlton was as dominant as any pitcher who ever threw a ball. He struck out 13 while throwing 160 pitches in a 9-4 win over the New York Mets. Other wins included a four-hit, 1-0 victory over the Montreal Expos in mid-June. In July, while posting six victories, Carlton captured a 3-2, 11-inning win over the San Diego Padres and consecutive 2-0 wins over the Los Angeles Dodgers and Cubs. In the Dodgers game, Carlton gave himself the win with a two-run triple off Tommy John.

In one no-decision game against the Giants, he was relieved after falling behind 4-0 in five innings. But the Phils roared back with an

11-run seventh inning to win, 11-4, sparing Carlton from taking a loss.

In early August, he blanked the Cardinals, 5-0 and the Pirates, 2-0, thereby recording four shutouts in his last five wins. Against Pittsburgh, he struck out 12 and gave up three hits, which would be the first of two straight three-hitters and setting a Phillies record with 15 wins in a row.

Carlton won his 20th game on August 17 when he beat the Reds, 9-4, while gaining his eighth straight complete game. Four days later, his streak ended when he lost, 2-1 to the Braves in 11 innings.

Carlton then won seven of his next 10 decisions, three of which were 2-1 triumphs. One was a 2-1 win over the Cards and Rick Wise. He finished the season with an 11-1 verdict over the Cubs.

And what a season it was. Carlton was saluted all across baseball. Posting the record that he did while pitching for a terrible team was a unique and magnificent feat, one of the greatest ever achieved in baseball history.

Mike Schmidt - Four Home Runs in One Amazing Game (1976)

Playing for the same team for 18 years is a rarity, as is hitting more than 500 home runs in that time.

Mike Schmidt did both. He played with the Phillies for 18 years, the longest any player ever spent with the team. During that time, he had a career loaded with special achievements, many of which rank among the game's greatest feats.

A good example are the 548 home runs he belted in his career. In the history of baseball, only 15 other players have hit more homers; only 27 players have hit more than 500 four-baggers. Schmidt has more than Mickey Mantle. He has more than Lou Gehrig. More than Jimmie Foxx. Even more than Ted Williams.

Schmidt led or tied for the National League lead in home runs eight times. Only Babe Ruth won more home run titles (12). He led the league in slugging percentage five times and in RBI four times. He won six Silver Slugger Awards. And he is the Phillies all-time leader in 10 different career offensive categories.

Along the way, Schmidt was the league's Most Valuable Player three times. Before that, only two other Phillies players—Chuck

Klein and Jim Konstanty — ever won an MVP award. Schmidt was named to 12 All-Star teams. He led the Phillies to a World Series championship, to one other Series, and to three other National League postseason playoffs.

Schmidt finished his career with a .267 batting average. He collected 1,595 RBI, 2,234 hits, scored 1,506 runs, and had 4,404 total bases in 2,404 games. The numbers make Schmidt the greatest hitter in Phillies history.

"Mike was the greatest player I ever played with, and certainly as good as any player I ever played against," Pete Rose once said. "Just to be able to rub elbows with Mike for five years (in Philadelphia) made my career worthwhile."

Of course, the 6-2, 195-pound native of Dayton, Ohio, who attended Ohio University (where unbelievably he was a switch-hitting shortstop) wasn't just a great hitter. He won 10 Gold Glove Awards. When he retired, he owned 10 club fielding records. His defense, combined with hitting more home runs than any other third baseman, makes Schmidt arguably the greatest third sacker in baseball history.

Schmidt's many achievements earned him induction into the Baseball Hall of Fame in 1995, collecting 444 out of 460 votes on the first ballot. Later, he was named to two baseball all-time greatest teams, one by the Baseball Writers' Association of America and one by *The Sporting News*.

Because of his batting prowess, Schmidt was highly admired — and feared — by all his opponents. "He's given me many, many sleepless nights because he can beat you in so many ways," Los Angeles Dodgers manager Tom Lasorda once said. "He can beat you with the glove or he can beat you with the bat."

Even the great Mickey Mantle recognized Schmidt's brilliance. "I don't know Mike Schmidt, but I do know what he's accomplished," he said. "He's a heckuva player."

That showed not only in career achievements, but in single-game feats, too. Time after time Schmidt performed spectacularly. The most sensational, however, was the one on April 17, 1976, against the Chicago Cubs at Wrigley Field.

It had been a long time since the Phils were a pennant contender, but having put together a solid team in 1976, they had finally moved up among the top teams in the league.

In their fifth game of the season, the Phillies took the field at Wrigley Field in the first of a two-game series. The Phils had a 1-3 record, with Schmidt carrying a lowly .167 batting average and an overload of tension. Manager Danny Ozark dropped him from third to sixth in the batting order.

"Mike, you've got to relax," said his close friend and teammate Dick Allen. "Have some fun. With all that talent you have, baseball ought to be fun. Enjoy it."

With Steve Carlton on the mound and 28,287 in the stands, the Phils were ready to have some fun. But distress quickly emerged. After Garry Maddox hit a home run in the second inning, the Cubs jumped all over Carlton, scoring seven runs in the second inning and sending him to the showers. Then the Chitown squad added five more runs in the third inning to take a 12-1 lead. By the fifth inning, they were ahead, 13-2.

Meanwhile, the 26-year-old slugger had flied out to deep center field in the second inning and singled in the fourth. He came to bat in the fifth with a runner on base and Rick Reuschel on the mound for the Cubs.

Schmidt drilled a pitch over the ivy-covered left field wall to cut the Phils' deficit to 13-4. Two innings later, he slammed another homer, this time with the bases empty. The blast came in a three-run inning that cut the Cubs lead to 13-7.

In the eighth inning, it was time for the Phillies' uprising to get even more vehement. After Allen slammed a two-run single, Schmidt came to bat with two men on base and Mike Garman now pitching for the Cubs. Schmidt socked a long drive into the center field stands, and the Phillies now trailed only 13-12.

Four home runs by Mike Schmidt led the Phillies to an 18-16 victory.

The frenzy continued, as Bob Boone homered to tie the score. The Phils then went ahead when Larry Bowa tripled home a run and scored on Jay Johnstone's squeeze bunt.

The Phils now had a 15-13 lead, but it didn't last. The Cubs roared back with two runs off Tug McGraw in the bottom of the ninth to send the game into extra innings.

Now another Reuschel was on the mound for the Cubs, Rick's brother Paul. It didn't matter. With Allen on first, Schmidt lined Reuschel's first pitch over the wall in left-center field to give the Phillies a 17-15 lead. They then added another run on Dave Cash's sacrifice fly.

Trailing by three runs, the Cubs weren't ready to give up. They scored one run, but that was it. The game ended with the Phillies taking an 18-16 victory. They had tied the National League record for overcoming the biggest deficit to win a game.. With that win, the Phils went on to triumph in 51 of their next 69 games, building a 15 ½ game lead in August.

There were 43 hits in the game—24 by the Phillies—against 13 different pitchers. Rick Monday and Steve Swisher hit four-baggers for the Cubs.

> But the day belonged to Schmidt. He wound up with five hits and eight RBI, in what was the greatest offensive game of his career. His four homers marked the first time in 82 years a National League player hit four consecutive home runs in one game. Boston's Bobby Lowe did it in 1894. Schmidt, up to that point, was only the 10th player to have a four-homer game.

Schmidt viewed his storied accomplishment with his typical laid-back attitude. "I wasn't thinking of anything special when I was up there," he said about his last at-bat. "I was feeling good, and I was nice and relaxed. I don't think moving down in the order meant anything. The last swing was the best for me because I didn't try to be too fine."

Currently, only 18 players have ever hit four home runs in one game. The list does not include Hank Aaron, Ruth, Williams, Mantle, and many other noted sluggers.

The next day, Schmidt hit a two-run homer to help beat the Cubs, 8-5, and followed with solo homers in each of the next two games. He hit a two-run four-bagger in the 10th game of the season, and solo homers on April 12 and 26. He finished April with 11 home runs in just 14 games, tying the major league record for most homers in the first month of the season. He finished with 38 round-trippers and his third straight home run crown, as the Phillies won the Eastern Division title with a club record 101 wins.

In 1979, against the San Francisco Giants, Schmidt performed another notable task. Over a two-game period, he hit a home run in four straight at-bats, slamming the last one in his final at-bat. Earlier that season, he smacked a game-winning two-run homer in the 10th inning of a 23-22 victory over the Cubs. They were two of the magnificent feats achieved during a prodigious career that ended with his retirement in 1989.

Larry Bowa – A Record-Setting Year at Shortstop (1979)

There is no position on the diamond that demands more skill than shortstop. With the possible exception of catcher, a shortstop is the most important player on the field.

A shortstop must have both mental and physical talent. He must know where to play on each batter. He must make a quick decision on nearly every ball hit his way. And he must be able to field, throw, and run like no other position on the field.

Larry Bowa fits all these descriptions. He showed that during a 15-year career, 12 spent with the Phillies, earning a place as one of the best shortstops in baseball history.

Unquestionably, Bowa knew the requirements of his position. "You've got to have a strong arm," he once said. "Good hands are part of it. And your first step toward the batted ball is very important."

Knowing the pitchers and anticipating what trying to do, is another asset. Having the ability to go far to your left or right is yet another need, as is being prepared, which requires a lot of hard work.

"There's not a minute when you're not thinking about what you're supposed to do," said Bowa, known for his aggressiveness, hustle, and often wearing a dirt-marked uniform by the fifth inning. "And if you're not prepared, it will show up.

"If a shortstop isn't tired after a game, he didn't do his job because mentally and physically you're involved in everything," Bowa added. "A shortstop is the manager on the field."

Bowa posted fielding records that put him at the top of the list of shortstops who were baseball's greatest.

In 1971, his sophomore year, Bowa set a major-league record for the highest single-season fielding percentage, .987. That year, he posted 272 putouts and 560 assists in 843 chances—all career highs. In 1979 Bowa set a new record for shortstops with a fielding average of .991.

At one time, Bowa held the National League records for the most games played by a shortstop (2,222), the fewest errors in a season (nine in 1972), and the most seasons leading NL shortstops in fielding percentage, six.

A lithe 5-10, 155-pounder, Bowa set a World Series record in 1980 for starting the most double plays (seven). Bowa also played in five All-Star games.

Many of his records have since been broken. For instance, Bowa now stands 14th on the all-time list of career fielding percentages for shortstops (Omar Vizquel is on top at .985). Cal Ripken, Jr. bested Bowa's single-season record with a .996 percentage in 1990.

Nevertheless, Bowa, who made only 211 errors in 10,398 chances in 2,227 games, posted some spectacular numbers, which, at the time were regarded with awe and amazement.

Ironically, Bowa's glove was not the only thing that carried him through a sparkling career. He was also a very capable hitter.

On defense, Larry Bowa was one of the all-time leaders at shortstop. (Photo courtesy of the Phillies/Paul Roedig.)

Overall, Bowa hit .260 with 2,191 hits in 8,418 at-bats. His best years with the bat came in 1975 when he hit .305, in 1978 when he batted .294, and in 1981 when he posted a .283 mark. In 1971, he led the National League in at-bats with 650, and in 1972 he topped the league with 13 triples. Bowa also stole 318 bases, including 39 in 1974. He had 20 steals or more in nine seasons.

With the Phillies, Bowa, a switch-hitter who usually batted at the top of the order, hit .264 while playing in 1,739 games.

Hard as it may be to believe, as a youngster a career in the major leagues was not considered to be a part of Bowa's future. He was cut from his high school team three times, and was generally disregarded by scouts after he got back in the game and was playing at a junior college. Despite his increasingly apparent talent, Bowa was not chosen in the free-agent draft.

A native of Sacramento, California, he was, however, scouted by the Phillies and made a strong impression on scout Eddie Bockman. Eventually, Bockman called Phillies farm director Paul Owens and asked him to watch some films of Bowa.

> "I'll never forget it," Owens said many years later. "Eddie went out and rented some camera equipment. We went to a motel, and he put the bedsheet up on the wall. He started running films of Bowa.
>
> "I thought he was setting me up for a big bonus, maybe $10,000. I said, 'How much does he want Eddie?' He said, 'I think I can get him for $1,000.' I said, 'Give it to him. I can see that he can hit and field. And the stuff you rented damn near cost $1,000.' We ended up signing him for $1,500."

After four years in the minor leagues, Bowa joined the Phillies in 1970. After hitting only .150 early in the season, he finished the year with a .250 mark and registered a .979 fielding percentage.

At the time, Frank Lucchesi was the Phils manager. "The biggest thrill of my career," he told a writer some years later, "was sticking with Larry Bowa when he was a rookie. He had a great desire for the game. I could see that desire. Not everybody could, but I stuck with him, and he became a star."

It became readily apparent that Bowa was a decent hitter. But his work on defense created special attention from those who watched him play.

Bowa could go far to his right and far to his left. He threw the ball hard to first from just about any position. And he seldom made an error. In fact, in 1979 he played in 146 games and made just six errors in 683 chances. Nine other times he went through a full season making less than 15 errors.

As a Phillie, in addition to his then-record career .991 fielding percentage, he led shortstops with .987 marks in both 1971 and 1972, .986 in 1978, .984 in 1974, and .983 in 1977. In 1974, he participated in 104 double plays, and in 1971 he had 560 assists. For his career, Bowa ranks 11th in double plays (1,265) and ninth in assists (6,857).

Bowa played a key role in helping the Phillies earn spots in postseason play in 1976, 1977, and 1978. He hit .333 in the League Championship Series in 1978. And he hit .375 in the 1980 Series when the Phillies captured their first World Championship.

Over the years, the Phillies have had many outstanding shortstops, including Dave Bancroft, Dick Bartell, Granny Hamner, and Jimmy Rollins. As good as they were, however, none ever had a year in the field at shortstop like Bowa's 1979 season.

Bowa's career with the Phillies ended after the 1981 season when he became part of one of the worst trades in the team's history. Bowa and future Hall of Famer Ryne Sandberg were sent to the Chicago Cubs for mediocre shortstop Ivan DeJesus.

Bowa played nearly four years with the Cubs and part of one year with the New York Mets before retiring after the 1985 season.

Two years later, he became manager of the San Diego Padres. He piloted the Padres for two seasons before returning to the Phillies as a coach. He spent eight years in that post, then was a coach with the Anaheim Angels and Seattle Mariners.

In 2001, Bowa was hired as manager of the Phillies and won the NL Manager of the Year in his first year. He worked four seasons as the team's skipper, compiling a 337-308 record. Later, he served as a coach with the New York Yankees, the LA Dodgers, and again with Phillies before becoming one of the team's senior advisors.

Overall, Bowa has spent 54 years associated with major league baseball. His 35 years with the Phillies, including 29 years in the team's uniform, is the longest of any individual in Phils history.

Quite obviously, Bowa's best years as a Phillie came when he performed on defense at shortstop.

Tug McGraw – Strikeout Clinched First World Championship (1980)

Winning the World Series in 1980 ranks as the greatest moment in Phillies history. It was not only an electrifying event, it was the first time in 97 years that the Phillies won the storied Fall Classic.

Ninety-seven years. That dates back to 1883 when the franchise was formed. Until 1980, the Phillies had won only two National League pennants. But never a World Series.

That changed in 1980 when Tug McGraw struck out the final batter in the sixth game of the Series against the Kansas City Royals, in what was at the time the biggest strikeout ever recorded by a Phillies pitcher.

McGraw did it with a pitch that sent the 65,838 fans at Veterans Stadium into a massive celebration in the stands, which quickly spread through the entire Philadelphia area with wild jubilation that lasted well into the following morning. Moreover, the pitch earned McGraw a place among the Phillies most captivating heroes.

The Phillies had won pennants in 1915 and 1950. But they only won a combined total of one game in the ensuing World Series, losing four straight games in each one. Between those unsuccessful trips to the postseason, the Phillies had finished in last place 16 times, 12

No Phillies' strikeout was ever more memorable than Tug McGraw's in 1980.

times losing 100 or more games, while reaching the first division just once during a 31-year period from 1918 through 1948.

Never once during that period did they come close to winning a pennant. After the 1950 pennant, they didn't make the postseason for another 26 years until 1976, when they launched a streak of three straight postseason appearances. None, however, opened the gates to the storied battle between the National and American Leagues.

Finally, in 1980, it happened. The Phillies fielded a star-studded lineup that included Mike Schmidt, Bake McBride, Lonnie Smith, Manny Trillo, Pete Rose, Greg Luzinski, Garry Maddox, Larry Bowa, Bob Boone, and standout reserves Greg Gross, Del Unser, and Keith Moreland. The pitching staff was led by starters Steve Carlton and Dick Ruthven, and relievers McGraw, Ron Reed, and Dickie Noles.

McGraw, who pitched for 19 years in the big leagues before his retirement in 1984, was for many years one of the kings of the National League's relief corps. A 6-0, 170-pound left-hander out of Martinez, California, he broke in with the New York Mets in 1965 at the age of 20. As a Met, he pitched in 60 games once and in more than 50 three other times. One year, he had 27 saves, in another he had 25, and in 1969, was one of the key relievers on the Mets' stunning World Series victory.

McGraw was traded to the Phillies in 1974 in a deal that also brought unknown outfielders Don Hahn and Dave Schneck to the Phillies in exchange for outfielder Unser, pitcher Mac Scarce, and catcher John Stearns.

Beginning in 1975 through 1980, McGraw posted a record of 40-29 with 79 saves in 336 games. Even now, he ranks first on the Phillies all-time list in games finished (313), second among relievers in appearances (460), innings pitched (708) and wins (49), and third in relief strikeouts (483).

His career record includes 96 wins, 180 saves, and a 3.14 ERA in 1,516 innings over 824 games. He started 39 games, including three with the Phillies.

Renowned for a sense of humor and great enthusiasm, while he was with the Mets, McGraw had invoked the rallying cry, "You Gotta Believe," during the team's drive to the 1973 pennant, and he used it for the rest of his career.

In 1980, the Phillies finished first during the regular season, one game ahead of the Montreal Expos in the National League's East Division. McGraw appeared in 57 games, recording 20 saves, five wins, and a microscopic 1.46 earned run average.

In the final weekend of the season, McGraw struck out five of the six batters he faced in a 2-1 Friday night Phillies victory over the Expos. The next day, he earned the win in the Phils' clinching 6-4 victory in 11 innings.

> Tug was known for naming his different fastballs. One was the John Jameson. "I like my Irish whiskey straight," he explained. Another was the Peggy Lee ("Is that all there is?"). His Bo Derek pitch "had a nice little tail on it." He also threw a Cutty Sark because "it sails." When he threw a home run pitch, he called it a "Sinatra ball," in honor of the song, "Fly Me to the Moon."

The Phillies went on to beat the Houston Astros in the NLCS three games to two. They won the final game, overcoming a 5-2 deficit with a five-run eighth inning rally against Nolan Ryan, then blowing the lead, before breaking a 7-7 tie on an RBI double by Garry Maddox in the 10th inning for an 8-7 win. It was the Phils' fourth straight extra-inning game win. McGraw pitched in all five games, losing the third game in the 10th inning, and posting saves in a first game 3-1 win and a fourth-game 5-3 triumph.

The 1980 World Series was as hard-fought and thrilling as the battle with the Astros had been. The Phillies went up against the Kansas City Royals, winners of the American League's West Division by 14 games over the Oakland Athletics.

The Royals were led by an outstanding crew that featured star hitter George Brett, who had flirted with a .400 batting average through much of the season, plus standout hitters Willie Wilson and Willie Aikens and 20-game winner Dennis Leonard and AL save leader Dan Quisenberry on the mound.

The Phillies won the first game of the series, 7-6, behind a five-run third inning led by Bake McBride's three-run homer. McGraw, who would go on to appear in four the six games in the series, earned a save, allowing one hit in the last two innings and striking out Wilson to end the game. The win gave the Phillies their first World Series victory in 65 years.

The Phillies won Game Two, 6-4, with McGraw on the sidelines. They lost the third game, 4-3, in 10 innings with McGraw giving up two runs in the 10th to take the loss.

The Phillies lost the fourth game, 5-3, then captured a victory in Game Five, 4-3. McGraw pitched three innings, striking out five, and allowing just one hit. In the bottom of the ninth, however, he loaded the bases with three walks before retiring the side and getting the win.

That brought on Game Six. The Phillies built a 4-0 lead, with Carlton yielding just three singles over seven innings. With two runners on base in the eighth inning, Carlton was replaced by McGraw. He loaded the bases on a walk to Wilson, then allowed a sacrifice fly by U. L. Washington. After Brett beat out an infield single, McGraw retired Hal McRae on a ground out to second baseman Trillo for the third out.

The Royals trailed 4-1 when they came to bat in the ninth. McGraw fanned Amos Otis, but then loaded the bases on a walk to Aikens and singles by John Wathan and Jose Cardenal. Frank White was up next, and in one of the Phillies most famous defensive plays in their long history, hit a foul pop to Rose, who caught the ball after it bounced out of Boone's glove, for the second out.

Wilson was the next batter. McGraw, his arm aching from so much work, got to a 1-2 count, then blew a pitch passed Wilson for the third out.

The clock said 11:29 PM. The date was October 21. It was to that point the most famous time in Phillies history. With police and dogs surrounding the field, McGraw raised his arms and jumped toward the sky, while Schmidt raced in from third base to leap on a pile of deliriously happy players. The Phillies had won their first World

Series. After the game, McGraw told the media, "I don't think I've ever been more proud to be a baseball player."

Asked what pitch he threw to strike out Wilson, McGraw said, "a fastball. The slowest fastball in baseball history."

Why was it the slowest, McGraw was asked? "Because it took 97 years to get there," he said.

How right he was. It took 97 years for the Phillies to win a World Series in a game climaxed by what was then the greatest pitch in Phillies history.

Pete Rose - Set National League Record for Most Career Hits (1981)

There's an old saying, "records are made to be broken." That may be true in some cases, but it's false in others. Some records will never be broken.

For instance, Nolan Ryan's total of seven no-hitters will never be surpassed. Neither will Hugh Duffy's .440 batting average in one season. Or Grover Cleveland Alexander's 16 shutouts in one season. Or Billy Hamilton's 198 runs in one season.

For decades, it was believed that Ty Cobb's record for most hits in a career would never be eclipsed. The record of 4,189 hits was set in 1928, and for many decades no one threatened Cobb's mark. Eventually, some 57 years later, the record was broken when Pete Rose singled during a game in 1985.

Earlier, Rose staged one of the Phillies most acclaimed feats when he broke Stan Musial's National League record for most career hits. Rose did it on August 10, 1981, in a game against the St. Louis Cardinals at Veterans Stadium.

By then, the switch-hitting Rose had already become one of baseball's foremost performers. After spending three years in the minor leagues, he joined the Cincinnati Reds in 1963. He would go on to spend 16 years with the Reds, winning three batting championships. He tied or led the league in hits seven times, reaching a high of 230 in 1973. In 1978, he had a 44-game hitting streak. During that season, he became the 13th, and youngest, major league player to sock 3,000 hits.

Charley Hustle, as they called him, was named Rookie of the Year in 1963, Most Valuable Player in the National League in 1973, and MVP in the World Series in 1975. In 1979, he was named by *The Sporting News* as the Baseball Player of the Decade. And when he reached a salary of $750,000 in 1977, he became the highest-paid singles hitter in baseball.

Rose became a free agent after the 1978 season. When the Reds decided not to offer the 5'-11", 203-pound native of Cincinnati a new contract, he signed a four-year $3.225 million deal with the Phillies.

Rose quickly became a Philadelphia favorite when he hit .331 in 1979, passing Honus Wagner as the National League's all-time leader in singles with 2,427. The following year, 1980, Rose was one of the key players when the Phillies took their first World Series.

Rose's average slipped to .282 that season, but he started a rally that won the final game in the Division Series against the Montreal Expos, 6-4. Then he scored the winning run when he knocked over catcher Bruce Bochy in the fourth game, a 5-3 victory over the Houston Astros in the championship series. Rose wound up hitting .400 in the NLCS, won by Philadelphia in five games.

In the World Series, he drew national attention when in the ninth inning of the final game against the Kansas City Royals, he caught a foul pop-up after it had bounced out of the glove of catcher Bob Boone. The play gave the Phillies their second out. The next batter struck out, and they captured a 4-1 victory and the Series.

The play led former Reds manager Sparky Anderson to say that Rose "is the greatest competitor I've ever seen. He's a star, but he doesn't look down on people. He's the only man I've ever seen who really believes in that old cliché about giving 100 percent."

In 1981, Rose continued to give 100 percent, and it elevated him to a level that ranks him among the all-time greats of the game.

"It's almost impossible to play every game with intensity," Richie Ashburn said. "He plays every game, every time at bat, every pitch with intensity. Pete is a player for all seasons, all decades, all time."

Rose went into the season just shy of Musial's National League record for most hits in a career. On June 10, he tied the Cardinal great's record of 3,630 hits when he singled to center field, off none other than Nolan Ryan, in the first inning of a game against the Astros at Veterans Stadium before a crowd of 57,386. Ryan struck out Rose in each of the next three at-bats, but a three-run homer by Garry Maddox in the eighth inning sparked a five-run rally to give the Phils a 5-4 victory.

After the game, baseball was scorched with bad news. No agreement could be reached in a dispute between team owners and the players union, and the players went on strike. The strike lasted 60 days, and the Phillies missed 55 games.

The season resumed on August 10, and before a national audience and a boisterous crowd of 60,651 at the Vet, the Phillies met the Cardinals.

One day earlier, Rose had driven from Cleveland, leaving at 1:30 AM and arriving in Philadelphia at 9:15 AM. Then he got just five hours sleep before leaving for the ballpark. "I got lost," Rose told the press. "Don't make a big deal out of it. I feel fine. I'm strong as an ox."

With Bob Forsch on the mound for St. Louis, Rose reached first base in the first inning on an error by the shortstop and later scored on a wild pitch. In the third inning, he hit a grounder to Forsch who threw him out at first. Then he grounded out to second in the fifth.

Rose was the leadoff batter in the eighth inning. By then Mark Littell was pitching for St. Louis. Rose, batting left-handed, smacked a grounder between shortstop and third base. It was a hit—number 3,631. Musial's record was broken.

Pete Rose is joined by Stan Musial after breaking his NL record for career base hits. (Photo courtesy of Phillies/Paul Roedig.)

The fans stood and loudly roared their approval. Fireworks exploded from the Vet roof. Some 3,631 colored balloons were released. Players raced out of the dugout to congratulate Rose, who tipped his cap and hugged his son, Pete, Jr. And then walking out to the field came none other than Musial himself. The Hall of Famer cheerfully congratulated Rose in a show of great class and elegance.

The hit came in Rose's 12,886th time at-bat. Rose eventually scored on a single by Mike Schmidt. He grounded out to second in the ninth inning, and the Phillies went on to lose, 7-3, getting just seven hits.

After the game, reporters flocked to the locker room. "The whole thing about breaking records," Rose told them, "is the reaction of the fans. It was very special because it happened at home in front of so many Phillies fans. Musial being there was icing on the cake.

"There was no pressure attached to this record," he added. "It's not like a hitting streak. I needed one more hit, and it was going to happen. It was just a matter of where, when, the kind of hit, and the pitcher.

"You have to be durable and consistent," he said. "That's all I ever tried to be in baseball. No question about it, I wouldn't be in this position if I wasn't durable."

> While Rose was talking, a phone rang. The call was from the White House. "Mr. Rose, hold on please," the operator said. Soon, a voice came on the line. "Hello Pete, this is President Reagan calling." "Hey, how ya doing?" Rose responded. With those words, the room exploded in laughter. Rose would always be kidded for his comical greeting.

Rose went on to hit .325 for the season. He spent two more years with the Phillies, followed by a brief stint in Montreal and then a move back to Cincinnati in 1984. The next year, on September 11, before a crowd of 47,237 at Riverfront Stadium, Rose hit a fly ball to left-center field off Eric Show of the San Diego Padres. The ball landed for a single, and Rose had erased Cobb's record. He added a triple in the seventh inning as the Reds won, 2-0.

Rose played one more year before retiring at the end of the 1986 season. He had played 24 years in the big leagues, finishing with a .303 lifetime batting average with 4,256 hits in 3,562 games. Ten times he slammed more than 200 hits in one season. He wound up with 746 doubles, 160 home runs, and 1,314 RBI in an all-time record 14,053 at-bats.

Rose played in 17 All-Star Games and earned three World Series rings while playing five different positions during his career. It was a career in which his time with the Phillies played a historic role.

Mickey Morandini – Turned Phillies' First Unassisted Triple Play (1992)

Of all the defensive plays in baseball, none is more rare or more exciting than an unassisted triple play. It is a play that not only demands talent, but also requires timing and being at the right place at the right time.

An unassisted triple play is so unusual that there have been only 16 performed in major league baseball history. Of that group, eight were achieved by shortstops, five by second basemen, two by first basemen, and—hard as it is to believe—one by an outfielder.

The first unassisted triple play happened in 1909 by shortstop Neal Ball of the Cleveland Naps. After that, there wasn't another one until 1920 when second baseman Bill Wambsganss of the team by then known as the Cleveland Indians retired three Brooklyn Robins in one of the most famous plays of its kind. It came in the fifth game of that year's World Series, the only time the Fall Classic has ever had such a majestic play.

Along the way, the Phillies never had an unassisted triple play until Mickey Morandini etched his name in the history books on August 20, 1992. At the time, it was the first play of its kind since 1968 when shortstop Ron Hansen of the Washington Senators performed that feat.

Morandini's triple play was the first one in the National League since 1927. It was also the first time in the National League that a second baseman had collected three outs on one play, and only the second time in big league history one had performed that spectacular feat.

Mickey Morandini's unassisted triple play earned him a place in baseball history.

For Morandini, the play left a glowing mark on his 11-year career in the major leagues. During those years, the 5-11, 170-pound native of Kittanning, Pennsylvania spent nearly nine years with the Phillies, plus two with the Chicago Cubs and part of one with the Toronto Blue Jays.

He was traded by the Phillies to the Cubs for Doug Glanville in December 1997. After two seasons with Chicago, Morandini had a crazy year in 2000. First, he signed as a free agent with the Montreal Expos. Two months later without playing a game for Montreal, he purchased by the Phillies. Later that season, he was traded to the Blue Jays. After the season, he retired that winter.

A left-handed batter, Morandini was a graduate of Indiana University where he began his college career as a center fielder, then was moved to third base where in his senior year he was named second team All-American. He was also a member of the United States Olympic baseball team that won a gold medal in 1988 in Seoul, South Korea.

Drafted that year in the fifth round by the Phillies, Morandini, then playing shortstop, spent nearly two years in the minors, eventually getting moved to second base because of the presence of Dickie Thon at shortstop with the Phils.

Morandini was called up to the Phillies late in 1990. The following year, he spent the early part of season with the Triple-A Scranton/Wilkes-Barre Red Barons before getting summoned to the majors to stay.

During his time with the Phillies, Morandini carried batting averages of .292 in 1994, .283 in 1995, and .295 in 1997. He also hit .296 with the Cubs while drawing 72 walks in 1998. He wound up with a .267 batting average in 965 games with the Phils.

Usually batting near the top of the order, he finished his career with a .268 batting mark, playing in 1,298 games, swatting 1,222 hits with 32 home runs and 351 RBI. He stole as many as 26 bases in one season, had 172 hits in another, and slammed 40 doubles one year.

In addition to many clutch performances at the plate, Morandini was always a fine defensive player, too. He made errors in double figures only once in his entire big league career, never making more than seven in any other season.

His fielding averages were always in the .980s, once going as high as .993 in 1998, a year in which he made just five errors. In 1998, he recorded 404 assists, twice participated in 87 double plays, and once had a season high of 286 putouts.

A member of the National League's All-Star team in 1995, his unassisted triple play, though, was certainly as tough as any play he ever made.

The Phillies were facing the Pittsburgh Pirates at PNC Park. It had not been a good year for the Phillies; they would go on to finish in last place in the Eastern Division with 92 losses. Amazingly, the following season, the Phils would make it all the way to the World Series.

But on that day in 1992, Morandini captured the spotlight with the season's most glittering feat. Morandini's gem came amid a late-season surge during which he hit in 10 straight games and batted .349 over a 16-game stretch.

The Phillies had taken a 1-0 lead in the second inning on a home run by Mariano Duncan. Then, with the score tied at 1-1 in the bottom of the sixth, the Pirates came to bat against Curt Schilling. Andy Van Slyke led off with a single. Barry Bonds followed with another single to put men on first and second base.

Next up was Jeff King. He worked a full count before smashing a line drive. As he did, the base runners were on the move.

"It was a bullet up the middle," Morandini recalled many years later. "King really smoked it. I dove for it. I was just a couple of feet from second base."

Morandini made the catch, which he later described as the hardest part of the whole play, then touched the bag to retire Van Slyke. At that point, Bonds was only about five feet away from second base. Morandini took two steps and tagged Bonds to complete the history-making unassisted triple play.

"The whole thing took only about 10 seconds," Morandini said. "It happened so fast that I didn't have a lot of time to think about it. I just concentrated on getting to the bag for the second out. In the back of my mind, I knew I had a chance."

> That he did. And adding to the glory of the play, Morandini was able to do it with his parents in the stands. "I'm from the Pittsburgh area," he said, "so I got to do it in front of my family and some of my friends who were there."

Ironically, Morandini had never seen a triple play before, dating back to his days in youth baseball.

The Pirates went ahead, 2-1, in the seventh inning, but a home run by Dave Hollins tied the score in the eighth. The game went into extra innings with Pittsburgh finally winning in the 13th, 3-2, on King's two-out single that scored Cecil Espy from second base.

In their history, the Phillies have reeled off 34 triple plays, including eight that were executed by second basemen. Opponents have staged 32 triple plays against the Phillies.

Second baseman Randy Ready and first baseman Ricky Jordan performed a triple play for the Phillies in 1991 on a play that started with a line drive by Tony Gwynn. Prior to that, the Phillies had not recorded a tri-outer since 1968 when the play went from shortstop Bobby Wine, to second baseman Cookie Rojas, to first baseman Bill White.

One other noteworthy feat in Phillies history is that three triple plays were pulled off during the 1964 season.

Since Morandini's gem, the Phillies have had one more unassisted triple play. That was also achieved by a second baseman, Eric Bruntlett, in a game won 9-7 by the Phils in 2009 against the New York Mets at Shea Stadium. The batter was Jeff Francoeur, who later played with the Phillies.

Over the years, some of Morandini's gear, including his game jersey, have been on display at the Baseball Hall of Fame. His glove, though, is a piece of equipment that has been shown only briefly around baseball circles.

"It was my bread and butter," he said. Indeed it was. It played a major role in placing its owner in a very special group who has performed one of the rarest feats in baseball.

Mitch Williams – Drilled a Walk-off Single at 4:40 AM (1993)

Rare is the baseball game that gets done in the early hours of the morning. When it comes to completing a game, it's about as uncommon as any game can be.

The Phillies not only did that, but they did it in a way that ranks as one of the most unusual games in baseball history.

It was a game that finished at 4:40 AM. No other major league game ever finished at that time. To add to the incredible finishing time, the game was the second one of a doubleheader. Together, the two games took 12 hours and five minutes to play.

Equally incredible, the game was won on a walk-off single by relief pitcher Mitch Williams in his only at-bat of the season.

The unfathomable finish occurred on July 2, 1993 at Veterans Stadium in a game between the Phillies and the San Diego Padres. At the time, the Phillies held a 5-1/2 game lead in the East Division on their way to a National League pennant and a spot in their fifth World Series in team history.

Having just returned from a road trip, the Phillies took the field for the first game at 4:35 PM, the regular time for the start of the opener of a twinight doubleheader. There were three rain delays during the game amounting to a total of five hours and 55 minutes. "Did you ever go two hours between at-bats?" Lenny Dykstra said.

The game was finally over at 1 AM, with the Padres winning, 5-2. The actual playing time was two hours and 34 minutes. Terry Mulholland pitched five innings and took the loss. The left-handed Williams hurled three innings in relief, giving up a two-run homer to Fred McGriff.

Mitch Williams's dramatic hit won one of the Phillies' most memorable games.

By then, most of the original crowd of 54,617 had left the ballpark. The ushers had been released, too, although some 20 supervisors remained at the ballpark along with a 16-man crew of groundskeepers, who had pulled on the tarpaulin three times during the first game. It rained so much that one groundskeeper, Mark (Frog) Carfagno remembered that "I wore five different shirts that night."

"There are no rules or guidelines for canceling a game because it's late," recalled the umpires' crew chief Dana DeMuth. "It was scheduled as a doubleheader, and our job was to get it in. We treated it just like any other game."

Eventually, the second game began at 1:26 AM with Jose DeLeon taking the mound for the Phillies. The Padres scored three unearned runs in the third inning on a three-run home run by Craig Shipley. Then they added two more runs in the fourth inning to take a 5-0 lead.

By then, only about 50 original ticket holders were left in the stands. But several thousand other fans, hearing about the history-making event, had left wherever they were and come to the game.

Williams, a native of Santa Anna, California, had a personal version of what was happening. "I couldn't believe they were going to play a second game," the pitcher known as "Wild Thing" said. "I had no clue they would play.

"My father and mother had flown in that day from Oregon," he recalled. "They came with my family to the game, but they left after the first game. My dad stayed, but eventually he got tired and went out in the parking lot to my truck, which had a bed in the back. He got in the bed and went to sleep."

Jim Eisenreich's RBI single got the Phillies one run in the bottom of the fourth inning, then Ricky Jordan laced a three-run homer in the fifth. The Phils added the tying run in the eighth on a pinch-hit single by Darren Daulton.

In the top of the ninth, the 6-3, 180-pound Williams, one of the game's top closers, was called in for his second game of the night. He walked one and retired three in the ninth. Then in the bottom half, Mariano Duncan doubled to right and was replaced by pitcher Tommy Greene as a pinch-runner. Mickey Morandini followed with a walk. But then Padres reliever Trevor Hoffman threw a wild pitch and Greene raced to third. He then tried to score, but was thrown out at the plate with Hoffman grabbing catcher Kevin Higgins's throw for the out.

That sent the game into extra innings. Williams retired the side in order. Then came the bottom of the 10th. Hoffman, who would later become only the second major league pitcher (along with Mariano Rivera) to record 600 or more saves during his career, was still on the mound for the Padres.

Pete Incaviglia led off with a walk. Eisenreich followed with a single. Next, Daulton struck out. Then Williams came to the plate. He had to bat because the Phillies, who used 19 players in the game, had used all their position players. "I remember it perfectly," Williams recalled. "There was nobody else to hit, so I had to bat."

It was only the third at-bat of his career. In his first big league at-bat, Williams had hit a three-run, walk-off homer while playing with the Chicago Cubs. He would go on to bat just 16 times in his entire 11-year big league career, collecting three hits.

> "I loved to hit," he said. "But they paid pitchers to throw, so I never got a chance to hit. I told Higgins, who had been my catcher in A ball 'If he throws me a changeup, I'm going to hit you over the head with this bat.' He threw me a fastball, and I hit it."

Ingaviglia raced home from second base with the winning run. And the Phillies had a 6-5 victory in a game in which they collected just 10 hits while the Padres finished with only five.

The actual playing time was three hours and 12 minutes, although it had taken 12 hours and five minutes to play the two games. The clock read 4:40 AM. "At my age, it was well past my bedtime," remembered Phils manager Jim Fregosi.

Incredibly, five days later, the Phillies would play a 20-inning marathon against the Los Angeles Dodgers. The Phils won, 7-6, in a game that took six hours and 10 minutes to play. This one wasn't over until 2:20 AM.

The previous record for the latest a game had ever ended had been set in 1985 in a skirmish between the Atlanta Braves and New York Mets. That game had ended at 3:55 AM, with the Mets winning, 16-13, in 19 innings.

As soon as the run scored, fireworks were set off at the ballpark. As Williams headed into the clubhouse, fans stood and shouted, "We want Mitch." Up in the television booth, Richie Ashburn roared into the microphone that "this is a record that will never be broken."

"Because it was my only at-bat of the season, I wound up hitting 1.000," Williams said. "I don't think anybody ever hit 1.000 for the season before."

For Williams, who finished the twin-bill with five innings pitched, allowing no hits in the nightcap, it was his second win in five decisions. In what was his third and final year with the Phillies, he would finish the season with 43 saves while hurling in 65 games and posting a 3.34 earned run average.

Williams, who had pitched with the Texas Rangers and the Cubs before coming to the Phillies, would later work with the Houston Astros, California Angels, and Kansas City Royals. He finished his career in 1997 with 192 saves and a 45-58 won-loss record while toeing the rubber in 619 games, finishing 419 of them and posting a 3.65 ERA striking out 660 in 691.1 innings pitched.

Williams had been traded to the Phillies by the Cubs in 1991 for pitchers Bob Scanlan and Chuck McElroy in what was one of Phils general manager Lee Thomas's best trades. He racked up 102 saves, which is the fourth highest on the club's all-time list. He wound up with a 20-20 record and a 3.11 ERA in 231.1 innings and 200 games, 173 of which he finished. In 1991, he won 12 games in relief, which ties for the third highest among relievers in Phillies history.

No game that he ever won, saved, or finished was anything like the one he pitched on that incredible morning in 1993 when his walk-off single won a game just a few hours before sunup.

With his two special seasons, Curt Schilling joined an elite group of pitchers.

Curt Schilling – Two Straight 300-Strikeout Seasons (1997-1998)

Few things on a pitcher's resume are as highly celebrated as his number of strikeouts. A strikeout is something that helps to elevate a pitcher's status, and the more he has, the more highly regarded he becomes.

Strikeouts, of course, are hardly the only figures on a pitcher's record that earn him a place among the elite moundsmen. But they do play a major role in determining how effective a pitcher is.

Pitchers who strike out a lot of batters are not all that common. It takes a pitcher who can throw especially effective pitches to strike out a big league hitter. Firing a blazing fastball is also certainly a necessary skill.

If a pitcher strikes out 300 batters in one season, he earns a special place in the annals of baseball history. As evidence of how difficult a feat that is, only 19 hurlers since 1900 have fanned 300 or more batters in a single season.

Only nine of them have done it more than once. That list is led by Randy Johnson and Nolan Ryan, each of whom did it six times; Sandy Koufax fanned 300 or more three times; and Pedro Martinez,

J. R. Richard, Sam McDowell, Walter Johnson, and Rube Waddell each did it twice. Koufax holds the record with 382 whiffs in 1965.

Also on the list is Curt Schilling, who registered 300 or more strikeouts in three seasons. Two of those seasons came in consecutive years with the Phillies. That amazing record earned for him a special place in Phillies history.

Schilling fanned 319 batters in 254.1 innings in 1997 and 300 hitters in 268.2 innings in 1998. He also kayoed 316 hitters in 2002 while pitching with the Arizona Diamondbacks. Only five other pitchers —Johnson, Ryan, Koufax, Richard, and Waddell-- fanned 300 or more batters in consecutive seasons.

Among this distinguished group, the 6-5, 225-pound native of Anchorage, Alaska, where his father was doing military service, had the fewest walks during a 300-strikeout season than any of the other pitchers. He walked just 33 during the 2002 campaign.

With the Phillies, Schilling became the club's single-season strikeout leader in 1997 when he passed Steve Carlton's 1972 record of 310. Schilling's 1998 total of 300 Ks ranks third on the team's all-time list. His total of 1,554 is fifth behind Carlton, Robin Roberts, Cole Hamels, and Chris Short on the club's career strikeout list.

While with the Phillies from 1992 through 1999, Schilling posted a 101-78 record and a 3.35 earned run average. In 242 games, he worked 1,659.1 innings, allowing 1,444 hits, recording 61 complete games, and 14 shutouts.

Overall, during a 20-year career in which he was named to six All-Star teams, Schilling pitched for three years with the Baltimore Orioles at the beginning of his sojourn and then one year with the Houston Astros. After leaving the Phillies, he worked four years with both Arizona and the Boston Red Sox, where he retired in 2007 at the age of 40. Along the way, he played for three World Series winners, including one in Arizona in 2001 and two in Boston (2004 and 2007).

His career stats include a 216-146 record and a 3.46 ERA in 569 games. In 3,261 innings pitched, he struck out 3,116, walked 711, allowed 2,998 hits, and compiled 83 complete games while also recording 22 saves, mostly in the early years of his career (he had nine saves with Boston in 2005).

Schilling arrived in Philadelphia right before the start of the 1992 season in a trade with Houston for pitcher Jason Grimsley. A reliever and an occasional starter, Schilling fell under the guidance of Phillies premier pitcher coach Johnny Podres and manager Jim Fregosi, and was soon converted to a full-time starter.

In his first year with the Phillies, Schilling posted a 14-11 record while leading the team in wins, ERA (2.35), strikeouts (147), and shutouts (four). In 1993, he logged in with a 16-7 mark in 34 games, leading the staff with 186 strikeouts and 235.1 innings pitched.

That year, the Phillies won the National League's East Division title with their only winning record (97-65) over a 14-year period between 1987 and 2000. Although he had no decisions in two starts in the NL Championship Series against the Atlanta Braves, Schilling's 1.69 ERA and 19 strikeouts in 16 innings, including the first five hitters in Game One, earned him the NLCS Most Valuable Player Award as the Phillies captured the series, four games to two.

In their third World Series since 1980, the Phillies faced the Toronto Blue Jays. In Game One, Schilling lost, 8-5. But after a 15-14 Phillies loss in Game Four, he came back in the fifth game to gain a 2-0 decision on a five-hitter in what was the Phils' first postseason shutout.

The Phillies lost Game Six when Joe Carter's famous three-run homer in the ninth inning gave Toronto an 8-6 win and four games to two victory in the Series.

Injuries forced Schilling to the sidelines through much of the next two years, but he returned to go 17-11, 15-14, and 15-6 from 1997 through 1999. It was the first two seasons of that streak that etched Schilling's name in the record book.

With a sizzling split-fingered fastball that could go as fast as 96 miles-per-hour and left batters lunging at pitches in the dirt, Schilling played for two low-level teams in 1997 and 1998, the former posting a 68-94 record and the latter going 75-87. But that hardly mattered. Strikeouts dominated most of his games.

> "I'm not intimidated by anyone," Schilling said about his mental prowess on the mound. "I don't approach a game based on who the team that I'm facing is. I approach it more as one hitter at a time. I do everything I can mentally and physically to prepare myself so when I step on the mound, there's no reason I should be caught off guard by anything that happens."

During the 1997 season, Schilling struck out 12 or more batters in a game seven times and had 17 double-digit strikeout games. Once, he fanned 13 batters in seven innings in a 9-3 win over the Florida Marlins. Another time, he whiffed 15 opponents in eight innings in a 3-2 loss to the Pittsburgh Pirates.

That season, Schilling made his first appearance in the All-Star Game, and struck out three in two shutout innings. Then in September, he fanned 16 New York Yankees in eight innings of work in a 5-1 victory. So dazzling was Schilling' performance, that Yankees owner George Steinbrenner immediately put him on his "want list."

"He's a horse, and he likes being a horse," Phils manager Terry Francona said that year. "I love the way he approaches the game. Obviously, he likes to be good at everything he does."

Having now past Carlton at the top of the Phillies season-high strikeout list, Schilling moved into 1998 at his usual fast pace. In a year when Mark McGwire and Sammy Sosa went on massive home run barrages, Schilling grabbed some headlines, too, with his strikeout performances.

During the season, Schilling struck out 12 or more batters six times, while recording 15 double-digit strikeout games. He fanned 15 batters while tossing a five-hit, 2-1 victory over the Atlanta Braves. Later, he kayoed 14 swingers in a four-hit, 4-1 win over the Chicago Cubs. He fanned 13 St. Louis Cardinals in a 9-3 victory, 13 Houston Astros in seven innings in a 4-1 loss, and 13 Chicago Cubs in seven innings in a 4-0 win. He also registered 15 complete games to lead the league, the most on the Phillies since Carlton notched 19 in 1982.

Later, Schilling said he was "proud" to reach 300 kayos. "I just wish it came in a win," he said.

Schilling had one more good season with the Phillies in 1999, a year when he started and lost the All-Star Game at Fenway Park. Then the following year, he was traded for four unheralded players to Arizona, where he teamed with Johnson to form a pair of strikeout wizards. Both passed the 300-strikeout mark in 2002, making them the only teammates to do that on the same team in the same season.

It turned out to be the climax of a fantastic career for Schilling as a strikeout specialist. Schilling's two 300-strikeout seasons with the Phillies were not only a brilliant accomplishment, but when it comes to Phillies pitchers, they put him in a class by himself.

Jimmy Rollins – Hit in a Team Record 38 Straight Games (2005-2006)

To be a shortstop in major league baseball, one must be an outstanding defensive player. You must get to those balls hit soft or hard, either straight at you, or to your left or right. And then make an accurate throw.

Over the years, baseball has had an abundance of shortstops who were superb fielders. The best ones could also hit well. Hit, run, field, and throw are what places a shortstop's name among the great ones.

Jimmy Rollins could do all the above, which is why he not only ranks among the greatest shortstops in Phillies history, but also as one of the best all-around players the team ever had.

Rollins spent 14 full seasons with the Phillies, dating from 2000 through 2014. He also put in one season each with the Los Angeles Dodgers and Chicago White Sox.

During his big league career, the switch-hitting infielder hit .264 with 2,455 hits, 231 home runs, 936 RBI, and 470 stolen bases. He also posted a career fielding average of .983 with 6,139 assists, 2,982 putouts, and just 154 errors in 9,275 chances.

With the Phillies, Rollins went .267-216-887 with 1,325 runs and 453 steals. On the team's all-time list, he ranks first in hits (2,306), doubles (479), at-bats (8,628), and most games played by a shortstop (2,058). He is second in total games played (2,090), total bases (3,655), extra-base hits (806), stolen bases (453), and plate appearances (9,511), and third in runs, singles (1,500), and triples (111). He also scored more than 100 runs in four straight seasons and hit 40 or more doubles in four seasons.

Rollins was named the National League's Most Valuable Player in 2007. He won four Gold Glove Awards, was named to three All-Star teams, won a Silver Slugger Award, the Roberto Clemente Award, and was a key member of five consecutive East Division champions and the 2008 World Series winner.

Jimmy Rollins's streak broke a team record that had stood since 1899. (Photo courtesy of Phillies/Miles Kennedy.)

When Rollins crunched a single off Chicago Cubs pitcher Edwin Jackson on June 14, 2014, it set a new Phillies record for most hits in a career and ignited a jubilant celebration among 32,524 fans at

Citizens Bank Park. They stood and clapped as Rollins waved to them from first base.

Mike Schmidt, who had held the record with 2,234 hits, and like Rollins was a second-round draft choice, was there to congratulate the new record-holder. He came down the first base line and held up Rollins' arm as fireworks exploded. "Congratulations. It couldn't have happened to a better guy," Schmidt said.

"I knew he was going to be here, but I didn't know he was going to have a part in it," Rollins said. "That was pretty nice. That was a surprise."

It was a major achievement for Rollins. The 5-7, 175-pound infielder was truly a dazzling player. But along with his eminent numbers, he also had one other feat that that put him in a class by himself.

Rollins is the owner of the Phillies' longest hitting streak of all time. In 2005 and early 2006, he hit in 38 straight games. That broke the previous club record of hitting in 31 consecutive games set in 1899 by Ed Delahanty, but it was the longest streak ever performed by a major league shortstop, as well as the eighth-longest streak in major league history.

The streak was well short of Joe DiMaggio's all-time MLB record of hitting in 56 straight games in 1941. But it put Rollins in a class with Wee Willie Keeler (45 in 1896-97), Pete Rose (44 in 1978), Bill Dahlen (42 in 1894), George Sisler (41 in 1922), Ty Cobb (40 in 1911), and the last one to join that group, Paul Molitor (39 in 1987).

That's an amazing group to be part of. And it added an accomplishment to Rollins's impressive resume.

Rollins had no greater compliment than the one that came from Phils manager Charlie Manuel. Putting Rollins in a class with Derek Jeter, Alex Rodriguez, and Nomar Garciaparra, Manuel told ESPN that "Jimmy sits there with those guys. When his offense is up there, it's tremendous. He does everything defensively you can ask of a guy."

Rollins's streak was especially difficult because it spread over two seasons. That meant that he had to sit and wait during the long winter months before resuming the run as soon as the new season began.

The 2005 season had not begun very well for Jimmy. He was hitting just .259 during the first half of the season, and when the streak began on August 23, his average was in the low .200s. Quite obviously, the streak, Rollins said, "wasn't something I was thinking about."

Coincidentally, the streak was launched near Rollins's Oakland, California birthplace. Playing in San Francisco, Rollins slapped a ninth-inning RBI double off the Giants' pitcher Brian Cooper in a 10-2 Phillies win.

Rollins followed that with three more one-hit games before lacing two hits in a 10-5 loss to the Arizona Diamondbacks. The next game was a two-hit game, starting with a first-inning double off of the New York Mets' Pedro Martinez; then six straight one-hit games, one of which was a double off the Houston Astros' Brad Lidge in the midst of a five-game Phillies losing streak in early September.

In the 14th game of the streak, a 7-6 loss to the Houston Astros, Rollins scored his first three-hit game. He followed that with three hits in two of the next three games, then poked one hit in the next two games. He bounced back with three straight three-hit games. The last one, coming on September 16 against the Marlins in the 22d game of the streak, included a home run, a double, four RBI, and four runs scored in a 13-3 Phils victory.

From that point on, Rollins had just five one-hit games during the closing month of the season. He had two games in which he belted three hits and six games when he socked two hits. He led off with a homer in two of those games. Rollins set a Phillies record on September 27 when got a hit in his 32nd straight game, against Juan Padilla of the New York Mets.

The season ended on October 2 with Rollins banging two hits in a 9-3 win over the St. Louis Cardinals. The victory gave the Phillies a final record of 88-74 and a second-place finish in the East Division, with Rollins slugging hits in 36 games in a row.

During his streak, the Phillies posted a 21-15 record with Rollins hitting .379, which carried his batting average for the season to .290. Rollins finished the campaign with 196 hits, which included 12 home runs, 38 doubles, 11 triples, and 115 runs scored.

After six months off, the streak continued in the opening game in 2006 when Rollins doubled off Adam Wainwright in a 13-5 victory for the Cardinals. The following night, another double off the Cards' Mark Mulder raised Rollins' record to hits in 38 straight games.

That, however, was the end of the streak. The next day, he failed to get a hit in another game against the Cardinals at Citizens Bank Park. Nevertheless, Rollins had become a major part of Phillies history.

"It was something that fell upon me," said Rollins, who finished the 2006 season with a .277 batting average and 191 hits. "It was a blessing to be a part of."

During the streak, Rollins hit .379 with 64 hits, including 22 doubles, four triples, and three home runs in 169 at-bats. He scored 36 runs, drove in 23, walked 17 times, stole 15 bases, and was hit by a pitch twice.

Rollins went on to have a glowing career-year with the Phillies in 2007. Rollins hit .296 with career highs in home runs (30) and RBI (94) and led the National League in games played (162), at bats (716), runs (139), and triples (20). He was one of the key players in the Phillies first of five-straight playoff appearances, including two World Series. In 2007, Rollins became only the sixth player in team history to capture a Most Valuable Player Award.

The following year, while hitting .277, he was a key figure in the Phillies first World Series victory since 1980. It was all part of a career during which the Phillies' sparkling shortstop had a masterful team record consecutive-game hitting streak.

Ryan Howard – Smashed 58 Home Runs in One Season (2006)

Since the advent of the lively ball and the outlawing of discriminating pitches roughly one century ago, the home run hitter has been by far the most beneficial offensive weapon in baseball. And any hitter who has the habit of slamming the long ball puts himself in a very special class.

Hit 50 or more homers in a single season, and that class becomes extremely limited. Altogether, belting 50 or more homers has been done just 46 times since Babe Ruth became the first batter to reach that level in 1920. Including the drug controversy seasons of the 1990s, 58 home runs had been surpassed only nine times before Ryan Howard reached that figure in what was the first an only time in their history that a Phillies player had reached that mark.

In so doing, Howard passed the Phils' record of 48 homers established in 1980 by Mike Schmidt. Jim Thome hit 47 dingers in 2003, and Schmidt had 45 four-baggers in 1979. The previous record of 43 homers was set in 1929 by Chuck Klein. He also ranks first in team history in grand slam homers (15), ranks second (six) to Schmidt (nine) in seasons with 30 or more home runs and 100 RBI, and he hit more career homers (382) with the Phillies than anyone but Schmidt (548).

During a career that extended from 2004 through 2016, the left-handed-hitting first baseman had a career batting average of .258 with 1,194 RBI in 5,707 at-bats. In 1,572 games, he swatted 277 doubles, scored 848 runs, and recorded a slugging percentage of .515. Howard was the fastest player in major league history to reach both 100 and 200 career home runs, and 1,000 RBI.

Born in Florissant, Missouri, Howard attended Southwest Missouri State University. He was the National League's Rookie of the Year in 2005 and was the league's Most Valuable Player in 2006, a year in which he also won a Silver Slugger Award. Joining Cal Ripken, Jr., he became only the second player ever to win Rookie of the Year and MVP honors back-to-back.

> Nicknamed "The Big Piece" and called "a very special player" by manager Charlie Manuel because of his gigantic home run production, the 6-4, 255-pound Howard was once asked by the author when was it that he first realized he was going to be an outstanding power hitter.
>
> "My mom started to tell me when I was a little kid," he said. "I was somewhere around seven or eight years old."

Others noticed Howard's early ability, too. "He had the physical skills and the baseball skills, and he handled himself very well," said Jerry Lafferty, then a Phillies scout. "He had good bat speed with great power. He had all the tools."

A fifth-round pick in the 2001 draft, by the time Howard first reported to the Phillies at the end of the 2004 season, he had spent all or parts of four seasons in the minor leagues. Then in 2005, he hit .288 with 22 homers and 63 RBI to win the top rookie award.

"At the time, I just thought of myself as a contact hitter," Howard said. "I knew that power was going to come. But I wasn't as concerned with that as I was just trying to meet the ball."

What followed in 2006 was one of the greatest seasons in Phillies history. In 159 games, Howard hit .313 and led the league in home runs (58) and RBI (149). He scored 104 runs and slammed 182 hits. He set club records for most intentional walks (37), most home runs in the month of August (14), and slugging percentage (.687). He trails only Chuck Klein (170) and Sam Thompson (165) for most RBI in one season by a Phillies slugger.

During the season, Howard had six two-home run games and one three-homer outing, tying Dick Allen and later Chase Utley for most multi-homer games in a season for the Phils. In 50 games, he hit at least one four-bagger. Thirteen times he had three or more RBI in a single game, and three times he had four RBI in a game. Over a nine-game stretch in late May, he socked one homer in six of the nine games, while driving in at least one run in nine straight. He also won the Home Run Derby at the 2006 All-Star Game.

At one point during the season, he hit in 14 straight games. Once he walked five times in a game. He homered in four straight games. In another game, he hit a pinch-hit homer that won the game in extra innings.

On June 20, he had one of his greatest games when he collected seven RBI with two home runs and a triple in a 9-7 loss to the New York Yankees. His first homer off Mike Mussina flew 437-feet into the third deck in right field, making him the first player ever to hit a ball into the third deck at Citizens Bank Park.

On August 31, he passed Schmidt's record with a home run that carried well into the upper deck at RFK Stadium in Washington, D.C.

On September 3, he had another memorable game when he smacked three consecutive home runs on nine pitches, a single, and drove in four runs in an 8-7 victory over the Atlanta Braves. At the time,

The 58 home runs hit by Ryan Howard set an all-time Phillies record. (Photo courtesy of Phillies/Miles Kennedy.)

Howard became the 23rd player to reach 50 home runs in one season. He also became the first major leaguer since Ralph Kiner in 1947 to hit 50 or more homers in his sophomore season.

With nine games left in the season, and Howard needing two homers to reach 60, he got 10 hits and walked 10 times (six intentional), but no homers.

"Someday in the off-season when I look back at this season," Howard said, "it will be special. I try to stay locked in and try to win games. One day, I'll wake up and realize what happened."

> Howard finished the season with home runs in 16 of the 19 ballparks in which he played. He hit 28 homers that either won or tied a game. He smacked 16 four-baggers off left-handed pitchers, and 27 homers to the opposite field. His best inning was the sixth when he walloped 13 balls out of the park. In games when he homered, the Phillies posted a 32-18 record.

"You hear talk about the ballpark we play in," Manuel said. "Honestly, it doesn't matter where Ryan plays. His home runs are legitimate."

Howard continued his stunning career in 2007. After signing a contract for $900,000, he battled through several injuries to hit 47 homers with 136 RBI and a batting average of .268. Then in 2008, he again won the home run title with 48 and the RBI crown with 146, while registering a batting average of .251 and playing in all 162 games. That year, the Phillies won their first World Series since 1980, with Howard hitting .286 with three homers and six RBI in the Series.

The following season, having signed a three-year contract for $54 million, Howard hit .279 with 45 home runs and tying for the league lead in RBI with 141. He then went .276-31-108 in 2010 and .253-33-116 in 2011. That year, he set club records for most consecutive seasons (six) with 100 or more RBI and most straight seasons (six) with at least 30 homers and 100 RBI.

Howard's last year was in 2016. In his final game as a Phillie, he was honored by the team and 35,935 fans.

"We had some good runs, didn't we?" he said when handed the microphone. "Philadelphia is always going to be my home. "I want to thank you (the fans) because I've grown up with all of you."

Phillies players were especially flattering in their comments about Howard. "Ryan, on countless occasions, put us on his back and carried us to the finish line," Utley said. "He was such an important part of our success, and I hope Philadelphia recognizes that."

To that, Jimmy Rollins added: "He loved the pressure and wanted to be the man at the plate when the game mattered most. During our run, we leaned on him many times. Ryan never stopped working to better himself and his craft, whether it was getting to the field early for extra defensive work or finding that sweet home run stroke. He was more than just a power hitter. He was a great teammate."

His home run totals were spectacular. None more so than his 58 four-baggers in 2006.

Brad Lidge – A Perfect Season as a Closer (2008)

Once upon a time, there was no such thing in baseball as a full-time relief pitcher. Relief pitching was a task performed by regular members of the rotation working between starts.

Although the first full-time relievers appeared in the 1930s, and more found places on rosters in the following decade, the position didn't really become an integral part of the game until the 1950s. From then on, relief pitchers became increasingly important, eventually reaching the point where teams now carry six, seven, or even eight relievers on their roster, including a specialist called a closer. Unlike in the past when a hurler would emerge from the bullpen and work numerous innings, in today's game hardly anybody spends more than an inning on the mound.

Meanwhile, in the early decades, there was no such thing as a save. Saves didn't become an official statistic until 1969 (after which historians went back in time to calculate saves among earlier pitchers.). Since then, rules have been instituted to determine what constitutes a save, as well as other stats for relievers, such as blown saves, save opportunities, and holds.

Over the years, the Phillies have had many outstanding relief pitchers. But no one put together a set of saves like Brad Lidge accumulated as the team's closer in 2008, the year the Phillies won their second World Series.

Lidge, a first-round pick of the Houston Astros in 1998, pitched for 11 seasons in the big leagues during a career that also included a brief stop with the Washington Nationals. He posted 225 saves and a 26-32 record, while pitching in 603.1 innings in 603 games (one as a starter). He struck out 799, allowed 492 hits, and recorded a lifetime 3.54 earned run average. He finished 368 games.

Brad Lidge did not have a blown save all season and postseason—in 48 opportunities. (Photo courtesy of Phillies/Miles Kennedy.)

Pitching for Houston from 2002 through 2007, Lidge had seasons in which he recorded 29, 42, and 32 saves. He also was one of six pitchers who participated in a no-hitter in 2003 against the New York Yankees. In 2004, when he struck out 157 batters in 80 games, it was the fourth highest single-season total by a reliever.

Acquired by the Phillies in a five-man trade with the Astros after the 2007 season, the 6-5, 210-pound righthander appeared in 214 games, collecting 100 saves, which ranks fifth on the team's all-time list.

It was the 2008 season, though, that earned the Sacramento, California native a place among baseball most prominent relievers. That year, Lidge recorded 41 saves in 41 save opportunities during the regular season, and seven more saves in seven save opportunities in postseason play.

Not a single blown save in 48 opportunities. During that time, Lidge appeared in 72 games during the regular season, posting a 1.95 earned run average and a 2-0 won-lost record. In 69.1 innings pitched, he allowed 50 hits while striking out 92 and walking 35. He finished 61 games.

> His amazing feat continued in the postseason when he registered two saves in the National League Division Series, three more saves in the NL Championship Series, and two saves in the World Series, including the most spectacular one in the Phillies clinching game. Altogether, Lidge took the mound in nine postseason games, working a total of 9.1 innings while yielding just six hits, one run, striking out 13 and walking three.

Lidge's regular-season record of 41 for 41 put him in second place on the all-time list of most saves without a blown save during the season. To that point, Eric Gagne of the 2003 Los Angeles Dodgers, was the only pitcher in major league history to place higher than Lidge with 55 saves. Since then, Jeurys Familia in 2016 with 51 , Jose

Valverde in 2011 and John Oxford in 2012, each with 49 saves, and Zack Britton in 2006 (47) have passed Lidge.

Lidge also became only the fourth pitcher in Phillies history to record 40 or more saves in one season, joining Jose Mesa (2001 and 2002), Mitch Williams (1993), and Steve Bedrosian (1987).

"It was clearly the greatest single season in the history of the franchise," said former Phillies general manager Ed Wade, who was then the Astros general manager who traded Lidge to the Phils.

Adding to this glowing record, from 2004 through 2009, Lidge had more strikeouts (605) and more appearances (433) than any other big league reliever. And since 1957, only three other times have major league relievers struck out more batters in one season than Lidge's 157 whiffs in 2004.

Ironically, Lidge's incredible 2008 season began with him on the disabled list for 15 days following knee surgery in February. After a brief rehab assignment with the Clearwater farm club, he rejoined the Phillies on April 5.

The closer, who was justifiably given the nickname "Lights Out," began the season with 12 straight saves. In his first 17 games, he did not allow a single earned run.

Lidge, whose fastball was clocked from 94 to 96 miles-per-hour, wound up the regular season allowing no more than one hit in 61 of his 72 games. At one point, he did not allow a run in 14 straight games. Then it was on to the postseason.

In the NLDS against the Milwaukee Brewers, which the Phillies won three games to one, he picked up a save in a 3-1 Phils victory in the opening game and another save in a 5-2 Phillies win in Game Two. Then in the NLCS against the Los Angeles Dodgers, which the Phils won four games to one, he got saves in a 3-2 victory in the first game, an 8-5 win in the second game when he struck out the side, and a 7-5 triumph in the fourth game.

In the World Series against the Tampa Bay Rays, Lidge got the save in a 3-2 Phils win in Game One. In the fifth game when the Phillies clinched the Series with a 4-3 win in a game that took two days to complete because of extensive rain, Lidge added the greatest save of his career, striking out Eric Hinske for the final out.

"We were the best team in baseball that year, and we just kept carrying it all the way into the World Series," Lidge recalled. "We were all very confident. Every one of us thought we were going to win the World Series."

When it was over, Lights Out dropped to his knees in what ranks as one of the most unforgettable scenes in Phillies history. Players raced to the mound to launch a monumental celebration.

"It was a complete feeling of elation," Lidge recalled. "I remember looking up, and saying, 'Oh My God.' At least, that's what I think I said. I was in awe of what just happened. You dream when you're a kid about winning a World Series, and then it happens. It's a feeling that will stay with you for a very long time."

Later, Lidge, who was awarded a four-year contract for $37.5 million, placed fourth in the voting for the Cy Young Award and eighth for Most Valuable Player. It was truly a remarkable season, unlike no other in the Phillies history of closers.

Adding to that feat, Lidge recorded saves in the first six of his save opportunities in 2009, stretching his regular season streak to 47 straight games. That put Lidge in third place on the all-time list of consecutive saves, following Gagne with 84 and Tom Gordon with 54.

That season, during which Lidge registered 31 saves, the Phillies again achieved a place in postseason play. In the NLDS against the Colorado Rockies, Lidge got saves in the third and fourth games of a four-game Phillies win. In the NLCS against the Dodgers, he added a save in Game One and was the winning pitcher in a 5-4 win in Game Four. With the Phillies losing in six games to the New York

Yankees in the World Series, Lidge didn't record a save, although he was charged with the loss in the fourth game.

In 2010, after spending half the season on the disabled list with an elbow problem, Lidge posted 17 saves in his first 18 opportunities, and ended the year with 27 saves in 32 opportunities, plus two saves in the playoffs against Cincinnati and the Giants.

Lidge's performance in 2008 when he collected saves in 48 straight opportunities, including the history-making clinching game of the World Series, holds a very special place in the annals of Phillies baseball. He was the first Phillies reliever ever to have a perfect season.

Chase Utley – Blasted Five Homers in One World Series (2008)

There are not many feats in baseball that are as celebrated as a player hitting a couple of home runs in a World Series. But if he hits five homers, he has gained a special place in the annals of the postseason classic.

Only two players have ever hit five homers in one World Series. One is Chase Utley. In 2009, he joined Reggie Jackson as the only player to perform this powerful use of the bat.

There are many ways to describe a major league ballplayer. That is certainly true in Utley's case. He was talented and tough. Focused, intense, humble, diligent, highly motivated, a hustler, and a hard worker. Most of all, he could hit, run, field, and throw, all with considerable ability.

Unquestionably, Utley was the best second baseman in Phillies history. In 13 seasons with the team—appearing in more games than any other Phils second baseman--he hit .282 with 233 home runs, 916 RBI, and a slugging percentage of .481. He was a six-time member of the National League All-Star team and a four-time winner of the Silver Slugger Award.

Overall, in a 16-year career that included four seasons with the Los Angeles Dodgers and part of one season with the Toronto Blue Jays, Utley had a career batting average of .275 with 259 home runs, 1,015 RBI, and a .465 slugging percentage.

A 6-1, 190-pound left-handed batter born in Pasadena, California, Utley was a physical fitness devotee who was always the first player to arrive at the ballpark, usually getting there about six hours before game time. Once there, he would work out relentlessly, hit in the batting cage, and study videos.

I respect the game, and if you respect the game, it respects you back," Utley once said. To that, the soft-spoken one-time UCLA athlete said, "I'm never really satisfied in the way I play. I always feel like I can play better. I try to put a game plan together on defense. Offensively, I just try to find the best way to win. My favorite part is just playing the game.

Phillies manager Charlie Manuel had his own version of Utley as a player. "He's one of the most prepared, one of the most dedicated players. He has the most desire and passion to play the game, and has a will to win more than any player that I've ever been around. He's a very special player and a pleasure to manage.

"I don't want to embarrass him or nothing like that, but sometimes I tell our players, 'Just play like Chase.' Because if you play like Chase, you've got a chance to be a pretty good player."

Owner of a short swing, who stood close to the plate and often got hit by a pitch, the thoroughly unegotistical Utley, hit more than 30 home runs in a season three times. Overall, he hit home runs in double figures 12 times, once leading the league with 131 runs and twice batting over 600 times.

His first hit with the Phillies when he joined the team in 2003 was a grand slam home run. He also hit in 35 straight games in 2006. And at the time, he was only the fourth second baseman in baseball history to homer 30 or more times in three different seasons and the third to have four straight 100-RBI seasons.

So highly regarded was Utley, that teammate, the great Roy Halladay, called him "the Derek Jeter of the National League. He's the driving force behind the team, and his preparation and desire are second to none," Halladay said.

Former Phillies star second baseman Juan Samuel once said to Paul Hagen of the *Philadelphia Daily News* that Utley is "a very special player. To me, there's no question that he's the best second baseman the Phillies have ever had."

Of all his standout years, though, it was the 2009 World Series that stands as the top performance of his career. That season, the Phils played in the third of what would be five straight postseason appearances.

Utley homered twice in helping the Phils win the 2008 World Series, the club's first Series victory since 1980 and only their second triumph in the Fall Classic in team history. The following year, they finished first in the East Division with a 93-69 record before moving into the playoffs and beating the Colorado Rockies in four games to win the National League's Division Championship. Utley homered in a Phillies 6-5 win in Game Three, while hitting .429 for the Series.

In the National League Championship Series, Utley hit just .211, but the Phillies captured four wins in five games against the Dodgers and set the stage for only their seventh appearance in a World Series.

Meeting the New York Yankees in the opener at Yankee Stadium, Utley got off to a stunning start when he hammered a home run off the Most Valuable Player in the American League Championship Series, CC Sabathia, on the ninth pitch of the at-bat.

The blow got the Phils off to an early lead, and three innings later, they added to it, thanks again to Utley. This time the rugged performer slammed a 96-mile-per-hour fastball into the seats to become the first major leaguer to hit multiple home runs in one World Series game since Reggie Jackson did it in 1977. Ultimately, the Phils won, 6-1, behind Cliff Lee's 10-strikeout, six hitter.

Chase Utley was only the second player to hit five homers in one World Series. (Photo courtesy of Phillies/Miles Kennedy.)

The Phillies lost the second game, 3-2, and the third outing, 8-5. In that game, Utley's streak of reaching base in 27 straight postseason games came to an end.

The Yankees won again in Game Four, 7-4, at Citizens Bank Park, but Utley returned to his personal home run derby. He hit an RBI double against Sabathia in the first inning, then smashed a home run in the seventh off Sabathia as the Phillies, with the aid of an eighth inning homer by Pedro Felix, fought back to a 4-4 tie. The Phils, however, wound up losing, 7-4, as Brad Lidge gave up three runs with two outs in the top of the ninth inning.

Down three games to one, it didn't look too good for the Phillies. But that didn't stop Utley. He was determined to keep the Phillies in the battle. And that's just what he did.

Facing AJ Burnett in the first inning, Utley clouted his first pitch for a three-run homer to give the Phillies a 3-1 lead. The advantage continued to increase, and the Phils led, 6-2, in the seventh inning.

Now facing Phil Coke, Utley crushed a 3-2 pitch into the right-center field seats at CBP. Adding a homer by Raul Ibanez in the seventh, the home team held back Yankees spurts to capture an 8-6 victory. Utley finished the game with two home runs, three runs scored, four RBI, a walk, and a stolen base.

The end for the Phillies, however, came two days later in New York when they plunged to a 7-3 defeat. Utley walked and scored on a home run by Ryan Howard, but there wasn't much more from him or the Phils.

Despite the Phillies loss, Utley had staged one of the greatest offensive performances in World Series history. Five home runs, eight RBI, seven runs scored, and a .286 batting average.

Not only did he tie Jackson with five homers, Utley became only the second player, joining Willie Aikens of the Kansas City Royals in the 1980 Series, to have two multi-home run games in one World Series. In addition, Utley's .795 World Series slugging percentage ranks sixth all-time, putting him ahead of big bashers such as Jackson, Babe Ruth, and Lou Gehrig.

It was truly a scintillating feat and certainly the greatest offensive achievement for a Phillies batter in the World Series.

Afterward, Utley spoke like a true champion. "I think we should be pretty proud of ourselves," he said. "I don't think that anybody should hang their heads. Winning and losing are part of the game. Obviously, we didn't accomplish our ultimate goal, but I'm proud to be a teammate of every guy in this clubhouse."

The reverse could be said, too. Everybody in the clubhouse had to be proud of a teammate who crushed as many home runs in one Series as Utley did.

Jamie Moyer – Oldest Pitcher Ever to Throw a Shutout (2010)

In the world of baseball, few pitchers are still toeing the rubber when they're in their 40s. Because most of them have been going out to the mound since they were teenagers, two to three decades of firing balls to the plate is more than enough of a load to put on one's arm.

Only 18 pitchers have worked in the major leagues when they were at least 45 years old. The list is led by Satchel Paige, who once pitched when he was 59 (three scoreless innings!) Jack Quinn, who hurled for the Philadelphia Athletics, worked until he was 50. Tied for third place at 49 are Hoyt Wilhelm and Jamie Moyer.

Behind them is a group that includes Nolan Ryan, Phil Niekro, Tommy John, Randy Johnson, Roger Clemens, Gaylord Perry, and Bartolo Colon. Each chucked the ball in the big leagues at or above 45 years old.

Of this highly distinguished collection of pitchers, Moyer holds some records unmatched by the others. In 2012, while pitching with the Colorado Rockies, he beat the Arizona Diamondbacks, 6-1, to become at the age of 49 ½ the oldest pitcher ever to a win a game, breaking Quinn's record set in 1932.

Jamie Moyer was 47 years old when he fired his remarkable shutout. (Photo courtesy of Phillies/Miles Kennedy.)

In addition to that performance, Moyer had another one that nobody would have thought possible. Pitching with the Phillies in 2010, he became the oldest player in major league history to fire a shutout. Moyer was 47 years and 170 days old. In that game, Moyer blanked the Atlanta Braves, 7-0, while allowing just two hits. The win raised his record to 4-2.

It must be said that although most of Moyer's memorable feats related to what he achieved at a certain age, these should by no means overshadow a sparkling career that included many other noteworthy accomplishments.

During a career that covered 25 years in the big leagues, he recorded a 269-209 record with a 4.25 earned run average. While playing in parts of four decades, the 6-1, 170-pound left-hander appeared in 696 games and pitched 4,074 innings. Moyer won in double figures 15 times and pitched in 50 different major league ballparks.

With the Phillies, Moyer posted a 56-40 record, playing with them from 2006 through 2010. He pitched in 123 games and recorded a 4.55 ERA. In 720.2 innings, he struck out 439 and walked 198.

Truly, Moyer had a marvelous career. It began in 1986 with the Chicago Cubs, then included time spent with the Texas Rangers, St. Louis Cardinals, Baltimore Orioles, Boston Red Sox, Seattle Mariners, Phillies, and Rockies. For nearly 11 seasons, he wore the uniform of the Mariners. He spent three seasons with both the Cubs and Orioles, two with the Rangers, and one each with the others.

A native of Sellersville, Pennsylvania, Moyer attended St. Joseph's University in Philadelphia before earning a degree from Indiana University. He spent parts of three seasons in the minors before heading to Chicago in 1986. Ironically, the first win of his career was a 7-5 victory over the Phillies. He later recorded his first shutout, retiring the first 19 batters he faced in 5-0 triumph over the Montreal Expos.

After several trips back and forth to the minors, Moyer blossomed with a 13-3 record in 1996 (playing for both Boston and Seattle). That started a streak of winning eight straight years in double figures, including a 20-6 mark in 2001 when he won 10 straight games, and a 21-7 record with a career-low 3.27 ERA in 2003, both with Seattle.

Moyer was traded to the Phillies in 2006, and in his debut became at the age of 43 the oldest pitcher to win a game in club history. Then in 2007, while posting a 14-12 record in his first full season with the Phillies, his 6-1 win over the Washington Nationals on the final day of the season gave the Phils the NL East Division title.

In 2008, not only the Phillies, but Moyer had one of their most memorable seasons. Moyer posted a 16-7 record with a 3.71 ERA while recording 30 or more starts for the ninth straight season. In a 20-5 victory over the Rockies, Moyer gained at least one win over every major league team. Moyer's wins were the highest on the Phils staff, and made him the second-oldest pitcher (behind Niekro at the age of 46 in 1985) to win as many as 16 games in one season. He also became the oldest Phillie ever to get a hit.

For the second straight season, Moyer won the game that clinched the regular season East Division title for the Phillies, working six innings, allowing just one run, beating the Nationals, 4-3. When he took the mound in the NL Division Series against the Milwaukee Brewers, he became at the age of 45 the second oldest pitcher to start a postseason game (he lost the game, 4-1). Quinn was the oldest at 46 in 1929.

One week later, Moyer became the oldest pitcher ever to take the mound in a NL Championship Series, a 7-2 loss to the Los Angeles Dodgers. Then in a 5-4 Phillies victory in the third game of their winning World Series against the Tampa Bay Rays, he became the second oldest pitcher (behind Quinn) to start a World Series game. In that game, Moyer worked 6.1 innings and yielded five hits and three runs, but didn't get the decision.

Moyer continued his fine work in 2009 when he posted a 12-10 record, giving him more wins (42) over the last three seasons than any other Phillies pitcher. At one point, he hurled a one-hitter over seven innings, capturing his 255th career victory. He also pitched in

30 games, giving him his 10th straight year of working in 30 or more games.

Phillies manager Charlie Manuel called Moyer "a total professional, and a team player."

"The biggest thing for me was to be competitive, and to perform at a level that gives our team a chance to win," Moyer said. "I didn't play the game for personal gain."

Moyer's 2010 season turned into one of the most memorable in his long years of pitching. And it wasn't just because of his age. With a fastball that was in the low 80 miles-per-hour, a stifling changeup, and a nasty cutter, Moyer was, as always, a highly effective hurler.

He started out the 2010 season by earning the victory in a 9-6 win over the Houston Astros. Then on May 7, he etched his name in the history books.

> At 47 years and 170 days old, Moyer became the oldest pitcher ever to toss a shutout when he beat the Braves, 7-0, firing a complete game two-hitter. A crowd of 45,349 saw the record feat at Citizens Bank Park.
> If it wasn't for Troy Glaus, Moyer would have had a perfect game. Both of the hits he surrendered were by Glaus, who poked leadoff singles in the second and eighth innings. Moyer struck out five and walked none.

While Moyer was working on his masterpiece, the Phillies hammered away at four Braves pitchers. After singles by Chase Utley and Ryan Howard, Jason Werth slammed a three-run homer in the third. In the fifth, singles by Placido Polanco, Utley, and Howard were followed by a two-run single by Raul Ibanez. Carlos Ruiz walked and Wilson Valdez socked a two-run single to climax a four-run inning.

Moyer's strong pitching continued through the rest of the game. For the seventh time, he retired the side in order in the ninth to cement the shutout. The scoreless game would be the 10th and final shutout in Moyer's career.

Moyer, however, was not finished recording great games. On June 5, he became just the third pitcher in major league history to win 100 games after turning 40 years old when he beat the San Diego Padres, 6-2. Then on June 16, he became the oldest pitcher ever to beat the New York Yankees, 6-3, with a five-hit, complete game. A little later in the season, Moyer gave up a home run to Vernon Wells of the Toronto Blue Jays to become the all-time big league leader in home runs allowed (506), passing Robin Roberts.

The season ended with Moyer posting a 9-9 record. Unfortunately, a damaged ulnar collateral ligament forced him to have Tommy John surgery that winter. Moyer had to sit out the entire 2011 season. In 2012, he joined the Rockies and worked in 10 games before retiring at the end of the year. It had been an outstanding career filled with many special achievements.

Roy Halladay – Fired Two No-Hitters in One Season (2010)

One of the rarest feats in baseball is pitching two-no-hitters in one season. Another one of the rarest feats in baseball is throwing a perfect game. One other rare feat is hurling a no-hitter in the postseason.

Roy Halladay did them all. It was one of the most remarkable feats in baseball and puts him in a class with some of the game's all-time greatest pitchers with one of the best mound achievements ever recorded.

In 2010, the Phillies right-hander threw a perfect game during the regular season against the Florida Marlins. Then in the National League Division Series, Halladay pitched a no-hitter, blanking the Cincinnati Reds.

Since the pitching mound was moved back to 60-feet, 6-inches from home plate in 1893, making all previous pitching feats from a mound just 50 feet from home plate far less significant, only five pitchers prior to Halladay's feat twirled two no-hitters in one season. That group includes Johnny Vander Meer — who threw back-to-back no-hitters in 1938 — Allie Reynolds in 1951, Virgil Trucks in 1952, Nolan Ryan in 1973, and Max Scherzer in 2015.

In 127 years, 20 pitchers have hurled perfect games. Only one other Phillies pitcher—Jim Bunning—ever threw a perfect game. And just one moundsman prior to 2010 ever threw a no-hitter in postseason play, that being the New York Yankees' Don Larsen's perfect game back in the 1956 World Series against the Brooklyn Dodgers.

In addition to these performances, only five pitchers have fired no-hitters more than two times in their careers. That illustrious group includes some of the greatest hurlers to play the game: Ryan, Sandy Koufax, Cy Young, Bob Feller, and Jason Verlander. Only 24 pitchers overall have hurled two or more no-hitters since 1893.

Halladay's spectacular season came in his first year with the Phillies. He had been traded from the Toronto Blue Jays, who had made him a first-round 1995 draft pick, in December 2009. He had been in the major leagues as a regular since late in the 2001 season after spending all or parts of seven seasons in the minors. Interestingly, in his second big league start in 1998, Halladay had thrown eight and two-thirds innings of no-hit ball against the Detroit Tigers, before allowing a pinch-hit home run to Philadelphian Bobby Higginson in a 2-1 victory.

The 6-6, 230-pound Denver, Colorado native, was noted for his fiercely competitive attitude and his relentless work to keep physically fit. He came to the Phillies with a 148-76 record, a Cy Young Award in 2003, and selections to six All-Star teams. In his career, he finished in the top five in the voting for the Cy Young Award seven times.

When he joined the Phillies, Halladay signed a three-year, $60 million contract. The Phillies were in the midst of the greatest era in club history. They would enter the National League playoffs five straight times from 2007 to 2011, go to three League Championship Series, and two straight World Series, one of which they won in 2008.

In his first start on opening day, Halladay beat the Washington Nationals, 11-1. He went on to post a 6-3 record before getting the starting assignment on May 29 against the Marlins in a night game in Florida.

Roy Halladay's no-hitters put him in a class with some of the greatest pitchers. (Photo source: Creative Commons 2.0, by Angela N.)

In his previous start, Halladay had yielded seven runs in an ugly five and two-thirds innings in an 8-3 loss to the Boston Red Sox. But the player they called "Doc" got some useful tips on a few mechanical problems from teammate Jamie Moyer and was ready to go in his next game.

Halladay threw 19 pitches in the first inning, but he escaped with no damage. He struck out five of the first nine batters and tossed no more than 12 pitches in any inning thereafter.

Several superb defensive plays helped the 33-year-old. Shortstop Wilson Valdez went deep in the hole in the sixth inning to stop a hard grounder by Cameron Maybin to throw him out at first. Shane Victorino raced to the warning track in center field to catch a deep fly by Mike Lamb for the first out in the ninth. After Wes Helms was called out on strikes, third baseman Juan Castro made his second outstanding defensive play when he went deep into the hole on a smash by Ronny Paulino and nailed him with an off-balance throw to first.

Halladay had a perfect game and a 1-0 victory. Even the 25,086 Marlins fans cheered as he walked off the field.

Overall, Halladay threw 115 pitches, 72 for strikes while mixing sinkers and fastballs in the low 90 miles-per-hour. He had six 3-2 counts and one 3-1 count. He struck out 11.

"I got in the groove early," he said. "It's hard to explain, but there are days when things kind of click and things happen. I was just trying to go one pitch at a time."

The new Phillies pitching phenom gave much of the credit for his game to catcher Carlos Ruiz. "I can't say enough about the game he called," Halladay said afterward. "After four to five innings, I just let him take over. It was a no-brainer for me. See the glove, hit the glove."

Halladay finished the season with a 21-10 record. It was the most wins by a Phillies pitcher since Steve Carlton won 23 in 1982. Halladay led the majors in innings pitched (250.2) and shutouts (four) and tied for first in wins.

A little more than four months after his perfect game, Halladay made the headlines again. Following the Phillies first-place finish in the Eastern Division with a 97-65 record, they entered the playoffs against the Reds, who were the National League's top offensive team, leading the circuit in batting average, hits, runs, home runs, total bases, runs-batted-in, and slugging percentage.

Halladay got the start in the playoff opener at Citizens Bank Park. With 46,411 screaming fans in attendance, Halladay, in the first postseason game of his career, blanked the Reds on no hits as the Phils won, 4-0. He just missed another perfect game, walking Jay Bruce on a 3-2 count in the fifth inning for the Reds' only base runner.

In the ninth inning, after Chase Utley caught a popup, and Valdez gloved a foul pop, the defensive play of the game came when catcher Ruiz jumped on a dribbler in front of the plate and threw from his knees to get Brandon Phillips at first.

It was the first no-hitter at CBP and Halladay became the only pitcher to hurl two no-hitters with the Phillies. Up to that point, there had been only eight no-hitters tossed by Phillies pitchers since the mound was moved back in 1893.

The Phillies ace struck out eight while throwing just 104 pitches, 79 of them strikes. Only four balls were hit to the outfield. Halladay also slammed an RBI single during a three-run second inning.

Manager Charlie Manuel, the winningest manager in Phillies history and the skipper during the club's glorious five-year run, called Halladay's gem "absolutely unreal." Ruiz said, "Everything was working. He threw anything on any count."

As for Halladay, his emotions were as always somewhat subdued. He called the game "surreal." He added, "I was definitely aware of what was going on. But pitching a game like that, being able to win comes first. That's your only focus until it's over.

> "It was one of the most electric atmospheres I've even been in," Halladay said, referring to the 46,411 people in the stands waving rally towels and making a deafening noise. Halladay said all that made him "more excited than nervous."

Halladay, who had made his seventh trip to the All-Star game, was a unanimous choice for the National League Cy Young Award, making him only the fifth hurler to win the honor in both leagues. He also finished sixth in the National League's Most Valuable Player voting.

The spectacular season was just the start of a triumphant four years with the Phillies. He logged a 19-6 record in 2011, placing second in the Cy Young Award voting.

Halladay posted a 55-29 mark with the Phils, before retiring after the 2013 season. He finished with a career record of 203-105 and a 3.38 ERA, and he was elected to the Baseball Hall of Fame in 2019.

Sources

Books

Lieb, Frederick and Baumgartner, Stan. *The Philadelphia Phillies*. G. P. Putnam's Sons, 1953.

Orodenker, Richard. *The Phillies Reader*. Temple University Press, 1996.

Shenk, Larry. *The Fightin' Phillies - 100 Years of Philadelphia Baseball from the Whiz Kids to the Misfits*. Triumph Books, 2016.

The Baseball Encyclopedia. Macmillan, 1997

Westcott, Rich. *Diamond Greats - Profiles and Interviews with 65 of Baseball's History Makers*. Meckler Books, 1988.

Westcott, Rich. *Great Stuff - Baseball's Most Amazing Pitching Feats*. Sports Publishing, 2014.

Westcott, Rich. *Philadelphia's Top 50 Baseball Players*. University of Nebraska Press, 2013.

Westcott, Rich. *The Champions of Philadelphia – The Greatest Eagles, Phillies, Sixers and Flyers Teams*. Sports Publishing, 2016.

Westcott, Rich. *The Fightin' Phils – Oddities, Insights, and Untold Stories*. Camino Books, 2008.

Westcott, Rich and Bilovsky, Frank. *The Phillies Encyclopedia*. Temple University Press, 2004.

Other Sources

Baseball-reference.com
Official Baseball Register, *The Sporting News*
Philadelphia Daily News
Philadelphia Evening Bulletin
Philadelphia Inquirer
Phillies Media Guides
Phillies Yearbooks
Phillies Report
Retrosheet.org

www.ingramcontent.com/pod-product-compliance
Lightning Source LLC
Chambersburg PA
CBHW030150100526
44592CB00009B/203